POLITICAL REALITIES
Edited on behalf of the Politics Association by
Derek Heater

PARLIAMENT AND THE PUBLIC

Second Edition

POLITICAL REALITIES
Edited on behalf of the Politics Association by
Derek Heater

POLITICAL REALITIES

Parliament and the Public

Second Edition

Michael Rush
Senior Lecturer in Politics
University of Exeter

Longman
London and New York

LONGMAN GROUP UK LIMITED
Longman House, Burnt Mill, Harlow, Essex CM20 2JE, UK
and Associated Companies throughout the World.

Published in the United States of America
by Longman Inc., New York

First published 1976
Second edition 1986
ISBN 0 582 35558 3

Produced by Longman Group (FE) Limited
Printed in Hong Kong

British Library Cataloguing in Publication Data

Rush, Michael
  Parliament and the public.—2nd ed.—
  (Political realities)
  1. Great Britain—*Parliament*
  I. Title II. Series
  328.41   JN549

  ISBN 0-582-35558-3

Library of Congress Cataloging in Publication Data

Rush, Michael, 1937–
  Parliament and the public.
  (Political realities)
  Bibliography: p.
  Includes index.
  1. Great Britain. Parliament. I. Title. II. Series.
  JN511.R87 1986   328.41   85-17072

  ISBN 0-582-35558-3

Contents

Acknowledgements

We are indebted to the following for permission to reproduce copyright material:

George Allen & Unwin Ltd. and University of Toronto Press for an extract from A. H. Birch, *Representative and Responsible Government*; G. Bell & Sons Ltd. for an extract from *Works of Edmund Burke*; Granada Television Ltd. for *The State of the Nation*: *Parliament* transmitted in July 1973.

We are also indebted to the following from whose sources tables within the book were compiled:

Social Surveys (Gallup Poll) Ltd., Gallup Polls in August 1976 and September 1978–October 1984.

Cover photograph: Camera Press

Political Realities:
the nature of the series

A great need is felt for short books which can supplement or even replace textbooks and which can deal in an objective but realistic way with problems that arouse political controversy. The series aims to break from a purely descriptive and institutional approach to one that will show how and why there are different interpretations both of how things work and how they ought to work. Too often in the past 'British Constitution' has been taught quite apart from any knowledge of the actual political conflicts which institutions strive to contain. So the Politics Association sponsors this new series because it believes that a specifically civic education is an essential part of any liberal or general education, but that respect for political rules and an active citizenship can only be encouraged by helping pupils, students and young voters to discover what are the main objects of political controversy, the varying views about the nature of the constitution – themselves often highly political – and what are the most widely canvassed alternative policies in their society. From such a realistic appreciation of differences and conflicts reasoning can then follow about the common processes of containing or resolving them peacefully.

The specific topics chosen are based on an analysis of the main elements in existing A level syllabuses, and the manner in which they are treated is based on the conviction of the editors that almost every examination board is moving, slowly but surely, away from a concentration on constitutional rules and towards a more difficult but important concept of a realistic political education or the enhancement of political literacy.

This approach has, of course, been common enough in the universities for many years. Quite apart from its civic importance, the teaching of politics in schools has tended to lag behind university practice and expectations. So the editors have aimed to draw on the most up-to-date academic knowledge, with some of the books being written by university teachers, some by secondary or further education teachers, but both aware of the skills and knowledge of the other.

The Politics Association and the editors are conscious of the great importance of other levels of education, and are actively pursuing studies and projects of curriculum development in several directions, particularly towards CSE needs; but it was decided to begin with A level and new developments in sixth-form courses precisely because of the great overlap here between teaching in secondary school and further education colleges, whether specifically for examinations or not; indeed most of the books will be equally useful for general studies.

Derek Heater

Preface to the Second Edition

It would be untrue to say that British politics has been transformed since 1976, when the first edition of *Parliament and the Public* was published. Nonetheless, important changes have occurred: in 1976 Britain was experiencing minority government for the first time since 1931 and since 1976 the emergence of the Social Democratic Party and the formation of the Liberal-SDP Alliance has had a significant impact on the party system. There have also been important changes in Parliament, including the replacement of the Expenditure Committee by fourteen departmental select committees in 1979 and an increasing willingness on the part of Members of Parliament to defy the party whips and force policy changes on the government. It would be premature to say that the Alliance has achieved its declared aim of "breaking the mould", but the mould is certainly cracked. Similarly, MPs may be more rebellious, though not to the extent that parliamentary government has been transformed, but British politics has changed and this new edition seeks to take those changes into account.

Once again I am indebted to the editor of the series, Derek Heater, who suggested a number of useful amendments to the manuscript. I should also like to thank Fay Burgoyne and Sue Ridler for their secretarial help, Brian Willan and his staff at Longman for their patience and prompt handling of everything connected with publication, and Nicholas Baldwin for providing up-to-date information on the House of Lords. Any errors that remain are, of course, my responsibility. Above all, I must thank my wife, Jean, who continues to tolerate and enthusiastically encourage my writing.

Michael Rush,
University of Exeter, April 1985

1 Introduction

Definitions are among the stock in trade of the academic and the more esoteric the thesis the larger they seem to loom. It may therefore seem inappropriate in a book about Parliament and the public to be concerned with what may appear to be academic trivia – after all, surely we all know what Parliament is? And are we not all members of the public? No doubt that much-loved tool of many academics, the opinion poll, could confirm for us that we, the public, do have an opinion as to what Parliament is. No doubt most of us would say that Parliament is the House of Commons and the House of Lords, though some might confine their definition to the House of Commons. Those with some historical knowledge might point out that in practice the Commons are more important than the Lords and that this is legally enshrined in the Parliament Acts of 1911 and 1949. Those with some constitutional knowledge might point out that in exercising its legislative supremacy – supremacy summed up in the phrase "the sovereignty of Parliament" – Parliament consists of the Queen, Lords and Commons. In a sense we would all be right, but the fact that we would all be right suggests that we need to look at Parliament in a context of reality: *the reality of politics*.

Unfortunately, politics is one of those words which has acquired a pejorative meaning in that it has become a term of distaste, even abuse. How often have we heard it asserted that this or that would be better if only politics were kept out of it or it were kept out of politics? Some matters are or should be, we are told, above politics. Politics is a dirty business, conducted behind closed doors and in smoke-filled rooms; the best that can be said for it by any apologist is that it is a necessary evil. As for politicians, can they not be dismissed by that cynical aphorism: a statesman is a dead politician?

But what do such critics mean? Are they really protesting against politics? Or is it, in fact, the *conduct* of politics that they find so distasteful? Are they not complaining about the behaviour of parties and politicians and governments? They may, of course, dislike all parties, all politicians and all governments, but in many instances a note of selectivity creeps in: *our* party, *our* leader is wise and statesmanlike, *yours* is foolish and partisan; scratch an objective man and you find a subjective man. A society's politics may be conducted wisely or foolishly and each of us may decide which we think it is, but this does not make politics itself good or bad. The existence of politics is a recognition that societies are by nature diverse. We commonly speak of society as though it has all the attributes of a single human being, but it is misleading to do so. This is not to deny the politician, the philosopher, the orator and others their rhetoric, but merely to point out that to use words like society in this way is divorced (sometimes perhaps for good reason) from reality. Societies consist of a multiplicity of individuals and groups whose interests are diverse and, in all likelihood, to some degree conflicting. Furthermore, societies are subject to change, and with change may come a divergence of interests leading to further sources of conflict. A crop failure, a flood or a pestilence are political matters just as much as the ability to explore space, victory or defeat in war, or a belief in liberty. Politics is concerned with the conflicts such problems create and with their solution. Politics, as Bernard Crick has argued, is "the activity by which differing interests within a given territory are conciliated".[1]

To define politics in this way does not mean that the *results* of political activity are right or wrong, good or bad, desirable or undesirable; on the contrary it is an acknowledgement of the fact that some individuals and groups will probably regard the results as right, good and desirable, while others will regard them as wrong, bad and undesirable: politics does not involve any obligation, moral or otherwise, to approve the results of political activity. It is a means of seeking to solve society's problems; it does not justify the solutions that may emerge, nor, for that matter, the means by which such solutions emerge.

In order to understand politics we need to know something of the problems for which a political solution is being sought; we need to know about the machinery that may be used or evolved to deal with these problems, what factors are likely to influence their solution, and what ideas influence both machinery and factors. Academically politics is not a self-contained and autonomous discipline, but an area of study whose limits are defined by the problem of conciliating "differing interests within a given territory". The factors which influence the solution of such problems are multifarious, and not "purely political" (whatever such a phrase may mean). Some are economic, some social, some historical, some philosophical, some physical, some psychological, some technological, some ideological, and so on. Not all will necessarily affect a particular problem; some will loom larger in some problems than in others. In some cases machinery may exist for dealing with a problem, in other cases machinery may have to be created, either because none exists, or as an alternative to existing machinery. The machinery itself, moreover, is operated by men and women and a pertinent factor may be who these men and women are and what ideas and opinions they have.

Politics is therefore much more than the activities of governments, whether local, regional, national or international. Of course in many cases governments have the power to decide what shall be done, but the power to decide does not determine the decision. Governments do not operate in a vacuum, nor is politics their prerogative; it is merely their sphere of activity. No matter what type of government is concerned, whether it be elected, appointed, hereditary, democratic, autocratic, totalitarian, or any other variety, it operates within a society and is subject to the pressures produced by that society.

Let us take the example of the building of a motorway in Britain. The actual decision to build a motorway lies within the power of the minister concerned and the Cabinet, although Parliament, through the House of Commons, has an indirect say in the matter because it has to approve the expenditure involved. In practice, however, the latter is a formality, since not only are most of the estimates (which authorise public expenditure) passed without discussion, but governments usually enjoy majority support in the House of Commons. But neither the minister concerned nor the Cabinet takes such a decision in isolation: civil servants will have been asked for and offered advice; various interests outside the government and Parliament, such as road hauliers, industrialists and trade unions may have been consulted or proffered their advice; the advice of experts in transport, engineering and other fields may have been sought; and so on. The very decision to construct a motorway affects the interests of many people, some nationally, some locally, some favourably, some unfavourably. For instance, various road users, private, commercial and industrial, would welcome the improved communications, and many of the inhabitants of towns and villages whose traffic problems would be reduced by the elimination of much through traffic would also welcome the decision. Others whose land might be needed for the motorway, who fear that the motorway might bring urban development in its wake, who favour the development of rail communications, who regard the car as an environmental monster, would deprecate the decision.

Even when the decision has been taken in principle the matter is far from finished, for the route has to be decided and the same sort of factors will affect this. Experts, such as civil engineers, traffic engineers, planners and economists may be consulted, but even assuming unanimity among these (which is unlikely), there remain other important considerations. How far should environmental factors, such as the proximity of towns, villages and individual houses, or the effect on the landscape, be considered? How many intersections should be built and where? Should large conurbations be bypassed or should an urban motorway be constructed? And, almost always a major factor, what constraints are imposed by cost?

The idea that some decisions are "political" and therefore taken by politicians and that others are "technical" and may therefore be left safely to the experts ignores the reality of politics. A decision is not political because it is made by a politician, but because it involves a choice between two or more possible courses of action, and because it seeks to solve conflicts between differing interests in society. Of course some decisions are primarily concerned with technical matters, but technical matters invariably have non-technical implications. A decision to erect safety barriers between the carriageways of a motorway is not simply a question of safety; it is also a question of cost: how much are we prepared to pay for greater safety? The design of an urban motorway is not simply a question for civil and traffic engineers; it is also a question of compulsory purchase and compensation, of traffic noise and pollution, and of people's homes and livelihoods: not only how much but *what* are we prepared to pay for the relief of traffic congestion and the improvement of communications?

There may be some advantage in leaving such matters to the technocrats and the administrators, to the benevolent neutrality of the expert, but in no sense does this remove them from the arena of politics. Various experts provide solutions to various aspects of a problem such as the building of a motorway, but such problems cannot be retained within the ambit of a single expertise. Moreover, it is ultimately a question of *values*. Experts may be able to tell us where to build the motorway and how much it will cost, but no one can tell us whether we are prepared to accept their advice or pay the price. As taxpayers we may shudder at the cost, but as road users we may welcome it; we may not welcome the prospect of living in its noisy shadow, yet we may welcome the relief it will bring to our residential streets; we may be the victims of compulsory purchase, but the beneficiaries of long-overdue housing. The conflicts are many; their solution is political.

Values are the lifeblood of politics, the basis of political action. Our attitudes towards this question or that are determined by our values, by what we believe about this or that. In terms of party politics, of course, it is a question of whether we hold Conservative, Labour, Liberal, Social Democrat or other views, or we may regard ourselves as liberals (as distinct from Liberals), socialists or Marxists, but it is not only these self-proclaimed "philosophies" or sets of values which are relevant; what we believe and think about much more mundane matters is just as important and often more so. Thus our hopes and beliefs about our jobs, our homes, our families and our friends and how they are affected by the world about us is fundamental to our political values. Our basic philosophy, be it liberal, socialist or whatever, may do much to determine our more mundane attitudes, but these mundane attitudes are also the foundation of our philosophy, and the interaction between the two is continuous. Furthermore, the line between fact and belief is blurred and the two may or may not coincide. What we *believe* to be the fact may be far from reality, but it will retain the force of reality because we believe it is so. To understand politics we need to understand what people believe, what motivates their political actions.

We cannot escape these beliefs when we come to examine political institutions and devices, for institutions like Parliament or devices such as an electoral system are not neutral pieces of machinery. They are the product of *ideas*, yet there is no simple causal relationship by which ideas shape institutions: both are part of a complex process by which ideas shape institutions and institutions shape ideas. Thus an institution such as Parliament may incorporate various ideas of representation, but these ideas may subsequently be modified by the experience of putting them into practice, changing both the ideas and the institution. Some ideas are matters of principle, others of expediency. For example, the existence of universal adult suffrage in Britain is now regarded as a matter of principle, but the actual age of majority which determines when people may vote is primarily a matter of expediency.

Parliament should therefore be seen as a product of political ideas – ideas about representation, constitutional responsibility and accountability, public opinion and democracy, ideas which are open to discussion and interpretation, ideas which are not immutable, but which have meant different things at different times and continue to mean different things to different people. It is foolish to believe that all would be well "if only we had the *right* machinery, the *right* political institutions". Parliament is not and cannot be neutral; no political institution is. We can describe its membership, what it does and how it works, but we cannot say categorically that Parliament is right or wrong, good or bad, desirable or undesirable. This may help us to decide whether we *believe* Parliament is right or wrong, good or bad, desirable or undesirable, for politics (and therefore Parliament) is ultimately a matter of opinion, whether it be informed or uninformed, organised or unorganised, that of the expert or the layman, the interested, the uninterested or the disinterested, the many or the few; and none has an inalienable right to prevail.

2 Parliament and politics

What is Parliament?

The terms "parliament" and "parliamentary" can be used in several different ways. "Parliament" is often used as a synonym for either the House of Lords or the House of Commons, although more frequently for the latter; "*a* Parliament" is the period between the proclamation summoning the House of Lords and the House of Commons to meet and the proclamation authorising new elections to the House of Commons and the summoning of a new Parliament; Members of Parliament, refers to members of the House of Commons rather than peers; the Clerk of the Parliaments is the head of the permanent staff of the House of Lords; the Parliamentary Contributory Pension Funds provides pensions for MPs but not for peers; the Parliamentary Commissioner for Administration (the "Ombudsman") works through MPs and reports to a select committee of the House of Commons; and so on. The fact that usage varies may cause some confusion, but it is important to understand what Parliament is and what it does.

"Parliament", Erskine May tells us in his manual of parliamentary procedure, "is composed of the Sovereign, the House of Lords and the House of Commons",[1] and this is borne out by the introductory words of most Acts of Parliament: "Be it enacted by the Queen's most Excellent Majesty, by and with the advice and consent of the Lords Spiritual, Temporal, and Commons, in this present Parliament assembled, and by the authority of the same, as follows . . ."[2] Yet, as every pupil is supposed to know, the Queen "reigns but does not rule" and the last time a monarch refused the royal assent to a piece of legislation was in 1707, when Queen Anne vetoed a Scottish Militia Bill. Similarly, the monarch has never regularly attended meetings of the House of Commons; the practice of occasionally attending the House of Lords died out under the later Stuarts; and the royal assent has not been given in person since 1854. The only occasion when the Queen now attends Parliament is the ceremonial State Opening, when she reads the Speech from the Throne outlining the Government's programme for the ensuing session of Parliament. The difference between constitutional fiction and reality is explained by the operation of what are known as conventions of the constitution. These are rules or devices of political convenience which have no legal force, but are widely accepted as binding by those engaged in political activity. Thus whatever her private views of legislation passed by the House of Commons and the House of Lords the Queen's assent is, by convention, a formality. Similarly, the government of the day is carried on in the Queen's name by ministers constitutionally appointed by her but who owe their office to the fact that they have the support of a majority of the members of the House of Commons.

The formal definition of Parliament also makes no distinction between the constitutional positions of the House of Lords and the House of Commons, but in practice the latter is the more important. This is not only because the powers of the Lords over legislation in general and financial legislation in particular are restricted by the Parliament Acts of 1911 and 1949, but in terms of *political* importance. The House of Commons is an elected body, whose composition determines which party (or parties) shall form the government of the day and provide the majority of ministers who form the Cabinet. The House of Lords is non-elective, consisting of hereditary peers, life peers, up to eleven Lords of Appeal and two archbishops and twenty-four bishops of the Church of England, and its principal function is to act as a revising chamber for legislation passed by the House of Commons. So far as Parliament is concerned political power resides in the House of Commons.

The difference between theory and practice is at its most important when we examine the concept of *parliamentary sovereignty*, which, in the words of A.V. Dicey, a leading constitutional authority in the nineteenth and early twentieth centuries, means that Parliament has "the right to make or unmake any law whatever . . . [and] no person or body is recognised by the Law of England as having the right to override or set aside the legislation of Parliament".[3] In theory Parliament could pass a law declaring that from a certain date all men shall be regarded as women and all women as men, but apart from the confusion that might arise the result would be negligible and the reality would remain. In practice the theory of parliamentary sovereignty is most important for the implications it has on the working of the constitution, but that is a matter we shall deal with in the next section. Its importance to an understanding of Parliament is that it forces us, or should force us, to look at the reality of what Parliament can and cannot do.

This is well illustrated by the arguments that raged over the Industrial Relations and Housing Finance Acts passed by Parliament during the Conservative administration of 1970–74. During its period in opposition between 1964 and 1970 the Conservative Party became increasingly convinced that the most effective means of dealing with strikes and other industrial unrest was to provide a legal framework for industrial relations. This would involve the estab-lishment of an Industrial Relations Court and a detailed code of fair and unfair industrial practices. The Conservatives were reinforced in their view by the abortive attempt of the Labour Government to introduce industrial relations legislation in 1969, which appeared to demonstrate the power of the "over-mighty" unions.

Over the same period the Conservatives also became convinced that council house rents, the level of which was controlled and which were in many cases subsidised at local level, should rise to nearer the market level. Both proposals were major items in the Conservative manifesto for the 1970 election. Soon after its election the new Conservative Government took the first steps in imple-menting these policies. Both the Industrial Relations Bill and the Housing Finance Bill were bitterly opposed inside and outside Parliament by the whole Labour movement, but by August 1971 and July 1972 respectively both had become law.

The majority of trade unions refused to cooperate in implementing the Industrial Relations Act and it was rendered largely inoperable. Not only was the Act repealed when the Conservatives were suc-ceeded by a Labour Government in 1974, but the Conservative Leader subsequently announced that his party would not seek to resurrect it. Although the refusal of the Engineering Union (AUEW) to obey the orders of the Industrial Relations Court brought it into direct conflict with the law, the refusal of trade unions to register under the Industrial Relations Act and their general policy of non-cooperation were not illegal, but their attitude did raise the important question of in what circumstances the "will of Parliament" could be properly defied.

This question was raised more starkly in the case of the Housing Finance Act in that a number of Labour councillors, outstanding among whom were those at Clay Cross in Derbyshire, refused to carry out the statutory obligations laid on them. Although their action did not prevent the implementation of the Act whilst the Conservatives remained in office, it did involve breaking the law.

In such situations the role of Parliament can become confused by the rhetoric of politics. Supporters of the Industrial Relations Act and the Housing Finance Act and others (who did not necessarily agree with the policies involved) deprecated some of the methods by which the Acts were opposed on the grounds that laws passed by Parliament should be obeyed. It was open to the opponents of the Acts to voice their opposition through public meetings, demonstrations, conference resolutions, petitions, writing to MPs, securing a hearing on radio, television and in the press, and so on, and to seek the repeal of the legislation. All of this they did, but, argued the critics, their opposition should stop short of defying the law, for the maintenance of the law – *the rule of law* – is the ultimate foundation of society. The law might at times be an ass, but it was no part of the argument of the upholders of the rule of law that the law was infallible, and machinery existed (ultimately in the form of Parliament) for removing any traces of asininity. It can be and was argued that not only does the breaking of the law bring it into disrepute, but so also does the refusal to cooperate in its implementation, even though this may not involve a breach of the law, as was largely the case with opposition to the Industrial Relations Act. The argument over the circumstances in which defiance of laws duly passed by Parliament can be justified has again become an important issue with the introduction of further industrial relations legislation and measures to curb local government spending by the Conservative Government under Mrs Thatcher.

As is often the case in such debates it is easy enough to provide extreme examples to illustrate arguments on both sides. Who can doubt that if sufficient people refuse to pay their rates or television licences then, at the very least, the law in this respect would become difficult to enforce? On the other hand, it is possible to conceive examples of laws which, even if they were duly passed by Parliament, would nonetheless be widely regarded as worthy candidates for defiance. Suppose, for instance, Parliament were to repeal the Habeas Corpus Act and other legal safeguards protecting the individual against arbitrary arrest, severely restrict the right to hold public meetings and impose a strict censorship on the mass media: the outcry takes little imagining. Cases like the 1971 Industrial Relations Act, the Housing Finance Act and the post-1979 industrial relations legislation lie somewhere between these two extremes and illustrate an important political truth.

In the sort of society that exists in Britain in which the *enforcement* of the law depends to a very large extent on its *acceptance* by those to whom it applies (even if they do not always agree with it), it is not difficult to render a law inoperable. Moreover, it is not necessarily a question of the rejection of a law by a majority of the people, or even by a majority of those to whom it is intended to or in practice applies, for very often it takes only a determined but active organised minority to render a law ineffective. The moral is that parliamentary sovereignty is limited by what, for the moment, we shall call public opinion, leaving whether it consists of a majority or a minority to later discussion. In other words Parliament should only pass laws which it can reasonably expect to be enforced. This does not mean that the acid test of a law is whether or not it is broken, since it may still be enforced, as was the Housing Finance Act following the refusal of the Clay Cross councillors to implement it. Nor should successful enforcement be equated with approval. For many years public opinion polls have found majorities *against* the abolition of capital punishment, but this did not ultimately prevent Parliament from going through with abolition. What it does mean is that Parliament should (and does for most of the time – it is always easy to be wise after the event) operate in the sphere of political reality not constitutional fiction.

When speaking of Parliament in this way it should not be forgotten that the Industrial Relations Act and the Housing Finance Act were placed on the statute book because there was a Conservative majority in the House of Commons; had Labour been in power they would not have been passed. Conversely, after Labour came back to power in 1974 not only were these acts repealed, but acts nationalising the aircraft and shipbuilding industries and increasing the rights and powers of trade unions were passed, none of which would have been passed by the Conservatives. What Parliament does, therefore, depends to a considerable extent on the distribution of seats among the parties in the House of Commons. With certain limited exceptions the *initiative* in what legislation is introduced lies not with Parliament but with the government of the day. Furthermore, the discipline and cohesion of the parties in Parliament is such that governments can normally expect to get their legislation through the House of Commons, whereas, for reasons we will consider later, the House of Lords rarely vetoes any legislation passed by the Commons.

Legislation is only a part of governmental activity, but it is the part which is most subject to regular and systematic examination by Parliament simply because the government must secure parliamentary approval for its legislative proposals and must submit them to a recognised procedure. Parliamentary examination of other areas of governmental activity is more haphazard, since many decisions do not require the specific approval of Parliament. In many cases legislation already exists giving the minister the necessary authority to take a decision, but in others ministers are acting under the royal prerogative, which consists of the residue of royal powers not superseded by legislation passed by Parliament, the exercise of which is not legally subject to parliamentary approval. As far as ministerial decisions are concerned the royal prerogative is most important in the conduct of foreign policy.

If ministers were obliged to submit all decisions for parliamentary approval Parliament would be overwhelmed with the additional burden of work that this would involve, even if it sat continuously throughout the year. As it is ministers are obliged to submit many of their decisions to Parliament in the form of statutory instruments, but in recent years the number of such regulations has been about 2,000 a year so that separate consideration of each instrument is impossible. In dealing with ministerial decisions and with policy generally Parliament has to be selective in what it examines. There is a practical limit to what can be debated on the floor of either House, to the number of parliamentary questions that can be answered, to what can be examined by committees, and to what can be voted upon; and that limit is *time*.

Of course Parliament, especially the House of Commons, possesses the ultimate sanction of denying the government a majority, either on a specific matter or as a means of forcing the government to resign, but this sanction is used only sparingly on specific matters and, notwithstanding the defeat of the Callaghan Government in 1979, rarely to bring the government down altogether. Even if it were used more frequently the fact would still remain that Parliament is *not* the government and does *not* govern. In a procedural sense Parliament does *decide* many matters, but most votes are on party lines, and many matters are not discussed at all. Whether Parliament in general and the House of Commons in particular should properly be described as a "rubber stamp" for government decisions is a different matter, for whether Parliament is effective or not there is no mistaking its basic political function: *to examine and question government policy and activity (or lack of it)*.

Parliament and the constitution

Unlike most other countries, Britain does not have a written constitution, but a collection of legally binding rules, some of which are written down in the form of Acts of Parliament and other legal documents, together with a number of conventions, which, as we have already noted, have no legal force but are widely accepted by those engaged in political activity. These rules and conventions have been developed over a long period of time and have been modified, adapted, interpreted and reinterpreted in response to changing conditions. Parliament is therefore the product of evolution not revolution; the product not of a moment in history but of history itself.

There was nothing inevitable about the development of Parliament. There was no smooth, steady progression from the Witanagemot of Anglo-Saxon kings and the Great Council of the Normans, through Simon de Montfort's Parliament of 1264 and Edward I's "Model Parliament" of 1295, on to growing strength under the Tudors and the triumphant struggle against the Stuarts, onward yet further to the building of a constitutional monarchy in the eighteenth century as a prelude to the extension of the franchise in the great Reform Acts of the nineteenth century, and so to the "Mother of Parliaments".

The origins and development of Parliament profoundly affect its present-day working. Neither in its structure nor in its rules and procedures is Parliament entirely a reflection of present-day beliefs and attitudes. Its origins and much of its development are "pre-democratic" and the roles of its constituent parts, whether conceived in terms of Sovereign, Lords and Commons or in terms of executive and legislature, have been subject to a remarkable process of adaptation.

Parliament owes much to the accidents of history. The struggles between kings and barons in the Middle Ages, in which both sides used "parliaments" to reinforce and legitimise their positions, created important parliamentary precedents such as consent to taxation and the right to seek the redress of grievances, but Parliament could easily have suffered the same fate as many similar institutions which failed to survive the Middle Ages in other European countries. Similarly, it should not be forgotten that after the defeat of Charles I there was a good deal of constitutional and political experimentation, that the period of the Interregnum between 1649 and 1660 was in many respects an interruption of Parliament as well as of the monarchy, and that the Restoration restored not only the monarchy but Parliament too. Even after the Restoration there was nothing inevitable about the development of a limited or constitutional monarchy. If anything the trend was in the opposite direction in other European countries, towards the establishment or consolidation of absolute monarchies. The role of the monarchy might well have been different if Charles II had not been so averse to "going on his travels" again, if James II had been as good a politician as he was a soldier, if the first two Georges had been more interested in English affairs, and if George III had been a better politician and not suffered from bouts of "insanity". But while the history of Parliament has been chequered and the development of the constitution irregular and spasmodic, there is a thread of continuity running through both, a continuity which may be summed up in the word *precedent*, and precedent is the foundation of the constitution.

Although various historical documents such as Magna Carta and the Bill of Rights, 1689, and Acts of Parliament such as the Reform Acts of 1832, 1867 and 1884 and the Parliament Acts of 1911 and 1949, provide an extremely important written element in the constitution, they do not enjoy any greater legal status than other laws. There is no special procedure by which the constitution is amended: all that is legally required is an Act of Parliament passed in exactly the same way as any other Act. Thus even a major structural change, such as the abolition of the House of Lords, can be achieved by passing an Act to that effect. Special amending procedures of the sort used in other countries, such as referenda or securing a majority of at least two-thirds of the members in the legislature, are designed to achieve a degree of consensus about constitutional changes and prevent arbitrary or partisan change by making the passing of constitutional amendments more difficult than the passing of ordinary laws. The British practice of allowing constitutional laws to be changed in the same way as any other law partly explains why historically the constitution has been so adaptable, but it does not mean that it is *politically* easy to change the constitution.

Governments are in practice wary about making major constitutional changes by legislation; the divisions over such changes have sometimes been very bitter and have taken place in an atmosphere of constitutional crisis, such as occurred at the time of the Reform Act of 1832 and the Parliament Act of 1911. Legislation forms an important part of the constitution, however, and much of it is taken for granted. Under the Parliament Act of 1911 no Parliament may last for more than five years, so that in practice a general election must be held at least once every five years. The right to vote is governed by the Representation of the People Act, 1984 (an act consolidating previous legislation) and the division of the whole country into constituencies, each returning one Member of Parliament, is governed by the House of Commons (Redistribution of Seats) Acts of 1949 and 1958. Elections have been held by secret ballot since the Ballot Act, 1872 (which has since been repealed and its provisions re-enacted in subsequent legislation) and elections are regulated by the Representation of the People Act, 1984. The House of Commons (Disqualification) Act, 1975, lays down the rules regarding membership of the House of Commons. The number of ministerial offices at the disposal of the Prime Minister is laid down in the House of Commons (Disqualification) Act, 1975, and the Ministers of the Crown Act, 1975, deals with the redistribution of functions between ministers and the alteration of their styles of address and titles. These are merely important examples; there are many more, but they are scattered throughout the statute book, although from time to time a series of Acts is repealed and re-enacted (or consolidated) under a single Act of Parliament. To a significant extent they provide the constitution with an important element of flexibility, but as far as the historical adaptability of the constitution is concerned *conventions* have been much more important factors, and conventions arise out of precedents.

There is no exact formula for determining when a precedent or series of precedents has become a convention. In a sense every royal and ministerial act, every resolution of the House of Commons, could create some sort of precedent, but a precedent alone does not create a convention. Let us take the example of the convention that the Prime Minister should be a member of the House of Commons.

The last person to hold the office of Prime Minister and remain a member of the House of Lords was Lord Salisbury, who retired from office in 1902. It is now clearly accepted that the Prime Minister must be a member of the House of Commons, although a short period outside the House, pending his election as an MP, can be tolerated, as it was in the case of Sir Alec Douglas-Home, following the disclaimer of his peerage on becoming Prime Minister in 1963. But the convention does not date from 1902. In 1923, following the resignation of the then Prime Minister, Bonar Law, Lord Curzon was one of the two contenders for the office. It is true that the fact that he was a member of the Lords and that there was no way in which he could disclaim his peerage and become an MP was a major factor in the decision to appoint Stanley Baldwin, but the fact remains that Curzon was seriously considered. Even so, 1923 created a precedent rather than established the convention, for in 1940, after the fall of Neville Chamberlain, a peer, Lord Halifax, was again seriously considered for the post of Prime Minister. In the event the precedent of 1923, the undoubted difficulties that Halifax would have encountered in being unable to address the House of Commons and be questioned by it, the objections of the Labour Party and the presence of a powerful rival in Winston Churchill, were more than enough to prevent his appointment, but the fact that he was not a member of the House of Commons was not alone sufficient to do so. The next occasion when there was no clear succession to the premiership was after the resignation of Sir Anthony Eden in 1957, but by this time the rule had been accepted and Lord Salisbury, grandson of the last peer to be Prime Minister and remain in the Lords, was considered sufficient of a non-contender to take soundings in the Conservative Party regarding Eden's successor.

The problem of deciding when a convention is created is perhaps best dealt with by begging the question and saying that a convention exists when a precedent or series of precedents is generally accepted as obligatory and is regarded as necessary for the effective working of the constitution at the time, which often means that no precise date can be given. Given the nature of conventions, this is bound to be the case, since constitutional precedents do not have the legal status of *judicial* precedents, which are regarded by the courts as binding. Thus the decision of a judge in one case will be regarded as binding by a judge in a subsequent case provided he is of the opinion that the cases are basically similar. Furthermore, there is no means by which conventions, unlike judicial decisions, can be legally tested. Unlike the United States, for example, there is no Supreme Court which can rule that certain actions are constitutional or unconstitutional. The highest court of appeal in Britain is the House of Lords acting in its judicial capacity through the Law Lords (the Lords of Appeal, the Lord Chancellor and any former Lord Chancellors), but the House of Lords can only interpret the law; it cannot decide what is constitutional and what is not. The application of conventions is therefore a matter of judgment for those involved. Conventions may be challenged, as when the House of Lords rejected Lloyd George's "People's Budget" in 1909, and from time to time situations arise in which there may be some disagreement over the interpretation of conventions.

Most conventions are accepted, no doubt reluctantly sometimes, and we can show the extent to which the constitution relies on them by describing how conventions provide the constitutional framework for British politics. Let us start by assuming that a general election has just taken place, the government party has been defeated, the main opposition party has won a majority of the seats in the House of Commons, and the Prime Minister has resigned. The Queen must now invite the leader of the new majority party to become Prime Minister and form a government. He, of course, agrees to do so and over the next few days consults his senior party colleagues (though with no obligation to take their advice), eventually returning to the Queen to "advise" her to appoint first the members of the Cabinet, consisting of the twenty or so senior ministers, and then all the other ministers who, together with the Cabinet, make up the government. In all rather more than a hundred appointments will be made and the Queen must accept the Prime Minister's advice in each case.

Furthermore, with only temporary and strictly limited exceptions, all ministers must be members of either the House of Commons or the House of Lords.

The Queen's legal powers are exercised in accordance with the advice of her Privy Council, which in practice means they are exercised by the Prime Minister and the Cabinet who are, for the time being, the active members of the Privy Council. The Queen has the right to be kept informed of what the government is doing and sees the Prime Minister regularly. She may express her views on any question, but she cannot override ministerial advice. The Queen must also give her assent to all bills passed by the two Houses of Parliament, or by the House of Commons alone under the provisions of the Parliament Acts of 1911 and 1949, which allow the Commons to override the rejection of a bill or part of a bill by the House of Lords.

Although Parliament is required under the provisions of the Triennial Act of 1694 to meet at least once every three years, in practice it must meet annually to authorise the expenditure of all government departments, presented each year in the form of Estimates, and to authorise the raising of any additional revenue necessary to meet that expenditure. The government continues to hold office as long as it retains the support of a majority of the members of the House of Commons. This does not mean that the government must resign following *any* defeat in the Commons – most governments, including those with large majorities, suffer some defeats during the lifetime of a Parliament – but if it is defeated on a major issue the government must either resign, or the Prime Minister must advise the Queen to dissolve Parliament and call a general election. The Prime Minister may also advise the dissolution of Parliament if he thinks his government should seek a fresh mandate from the electorate.

Ministers are not only drawn from Parliament but are responsible to Parliament for the conduct of affairs. This ministerial responsibility takes two forms, collective and individual. Collective responsibility means that the government as a whole, from the Prime Minister at the top to the junior whips at the bottom, are bound by the decisions of the Cabinet. At its most formal it means that the Cabinet is expected to offer unanimous "advice" to the Queen, but the ultimate operation of collective responsibility is that when the

Prime Minister resigns his whole government resigns. During their tenure of office ministers are expected to offer at least tacit support to the policies of the government (which means that they should not publicly oppose them), or resign.

Individual responsibility renders each minister responsible to Parliament for the conduct of his Department to the extent that the actions of civil servants are regarded as the actions of the minister, although a minister is not held responsible for the actions of civil servants who disobey or defy instructions or who act reprehensibly in circumstances of which the minister could not have been aware. Ultimately a minister may be forced to resign as a result of his own incompetence or the failings of his Department. Ministerial responsibility enables Parliament to call the government and individual members of it to account (*a*) by asking parliamentary questions, which ministers must normally answer, (*b*) through debates, in which ministers are expected to participate; (*c*) through committees, which may receive evidence from ministers, and civil servants; and ultimately (*d*) through the division lobbies, in which the votes of MPs are recorded.

The House of Commons, as we have already noted, is in practice the more important of the two Houses and it is generally recognised that in cases of conflict the Lords should ultimately yield to the Commons. This does not mean that the House of Lords should not amend legislation passed by the House of Commons, even when it knows that the latter feels strongly about the matter, but that if the Commons persist in their view the Lords should normally give way. This position has been partly modified by the Parliament Acts of 1911 and 1949; these enable the House of Commons to overcome the opposition of the Lords by passing the bill concerned in two successive parliamentary sessions, a practice dating from the 1949 Act which reduced the period of delay provided in the 1911 Act. In fact only three bills, including the 1949 Act itself, were passed under the provisions of the 1911 Act and none has been passed under the 1949 Act. The effect of the Parliament Acts is to give statutory support to the convention by providing machinery to enable the will of the Commons *ultimately* to prevail.

The Parliament Act of 1911 also limits the powers of the House of Lords over certain financial legislation, known as money bills, which must be passed by the Lords within a month of being received from the Commons, after which they go forward for the royal assent regardless. Money bills, certified as such by the Speaker of the House of Commons, are those which *exclusively* authorise public expenditure or the raising of revenue, and include the three annual bills known as the Consolidated Fund Bills Nos 1 and 2 and the Appropriations Bill (through which the Commons approves the government's expenditure proposals) and some, though not all, bills imposing taxation. In the latter case some bills imposing taxation also include other provisions which are not directly concerned with taxation and are not therefore defined as money bills under the 1911 Act. This more often than not includes the annual Finance Bill, which incorporates the proposals presented by the Chancellor of the Exchequer in his Budget. Thus the Lords rarely seek to amend a bill certified as a money bill, or the Finance Bill, but this does not prevent the upper House from debating financial matters and the Finance Bill in particular is usually fully discussed in the Lords.

The financial provisions of the 1911 Act gave statutory effect to the long-standing convention that in financial matters the will of the Commons should prevail. The financial primacy of the Commons is further emphasised by the fact that proposals involving changes in public expenditure or taxation must be introduced in the House of Commons. Of greater significance, however, is that any proposal for an *increase* (but not a reduction) in expenditure, or for an *increase* (but not a reduction) in taxation, or a new tax, must be introduced by a minister and not by a backbench M.P. This stresses not only the financial primacy of the Commons but, more to the point, of the government. It also brings us much closer to political reality and to the place of Parliament in that political reality.

Parliament and political reality

Control over public expenditure and taxation stresses the general primacy of the government over the House of Commons. Provided the government has a majority in the House of Commons it can ensure the passage of its legislation through the House of Commons and the approval of its policies, and, as we have seen, the will of the House of Commons normally prevails over that of the House of Lords.

The primacy of the government does not stem solely from the use of its majority but also from its power of *initiative*, especially in financial matters. Thus even in a situation of minority government, when the government must rely on the support of parties other than its own, the initiative remains with the government. The government must present proposals for expenditure and taxation; the government takes the initiative in major policy areas; the government oversees the work of the departments in Whitehall: in short, *the government is expected to govern.* Its task may be rendered more difficult by the lack of a majority or by a small majority in the House of Commons, but that from time to time, is a political reality for which the constitution makes no special allowance. In such circumstances the government may be forced by Parliament in general and the House of Commons in particular to trim its sails. Between 1964 and 1966, for example, when the Labour Government had a majority which varied between two and four, legislation nationalising the steel industry was postponed because two Labour MPs threatened to oppose it. The minority Labour Governments of March to October 1974 and 1976–79 were defeated on a number of issues and forced to accept amendments to major pieces of legislation, including budget proposals, trade union legislation and the proposals for devolution for Scotland and Wales. For part of this time the minority Labour Government was supported by the Liberals, having concluded the so-called "Lib-Lab Pact", which lasted from March 1977 until July 1978. In return for their support the Liberals demanded and secured a number of policy changes. Thus sails may be trimmed in anticipation of difficulty or defeat, or as a result of difficulty or defeat.

The conditions of minority government, or where the government cannot be certain of its majority, are those most favourable for the assertion of parliamentary influence, but in no sense does Parliament govern, although its influence may be decisive in a limited number of cases. There remains one further element to be fitted into the picture of political reality – that of party. The day of the independent Member of Parliament, untrammelled by party ties and proclaiming no party allegiance, is long past, and in the twentieth century almost all MPs have been party men. Moreover the great majority have been members of the major parties which have dominated modern British politics: first Conservatives and Liberals, and later Conservatives and Labour. It is true that recent general elections and by-elections have seen an upsurge in support for other (or third) parties, in the form of a Liberal revival and the emergence of Scottish, Welsh and Ulster nationalism, and, most recently, the emergence of the Social Democratic Party and the establishment of the Liberal-SDP Alliance, and that this support has been sufficient to secure representation for these parties in the House of Commons. Even so, the latter remains dominated by parties. This is recognised by the existence of several conventions. Thus the business of the House of Commons is arranged informally between the parties, primarily between the Government and the Opposition, although third parties are consulted from time to time, much depending on the extent of their representation in the House. The parties are represented on parliamentary committees in proportion to their strengths in the House and the nomination of members of committees is made by the party leaders through their respective party whips. The Speaker also recognises the existence of parties by protecting the rights of minorities in debate and, as far as possible, calling speakers from alternate parties. The increased representation of third parties may create a more fluid and possibly less stable situation, but no matter what form of government results, be it one-party or a combination of two or more parties, majority, minority or coalition, it remains *party* government.

Given the fact of party government it can be argued that the existence of parties, especially when one holds a majority of the seats in the House of Commons, renders Parliament a cipher, a rubber-stamp for government actions and policies, and it is pertinent to ask what the term "party government" means. Does it mean government by the MPs of the party in power? Most observers would emphatically deny this and maintain that for the most part MPs follow rather than lead, although there is more dispute over the extent to which they can and do influence their party leaders. Does it mean Cabinet or even prime-ministerial government? The British system of government is sometimes described as "Cabinet government" on the grounds that power is exercised by the relatively small group of senior ministers who form the Cabinet, which is constitutionally responsible to Parliament, but there are those who strongly argue that power is now so concentrated in the office of Prime Minister that we have "prime-ministerial government". The evidence is far from conclusive: few would deny that the Prime Minister is extremely powerful and that he has become more powerful in modern times, but it is doubtful whether his Cabinet colleagues should be cast in the role of political eunuchs.

Does it mean government by the party outside Parliament, whether formally through the party organisations, or informally through the parties' most powerful supporters? Arguments about the role of the party conferences, especially the Labour Party Conference, are perennial, and there are always those who claim to detect the sinister (or dexter, as the case may be) hand of Labour Party headquarters or the Conservative Central Office. Similarly, there are accusations that the Conservative Party is dominated by and beholden to "big business" and that the Labour Party is the creature of the trade unions, at the very least this is how the two parties see each other. But such arguments must be inductive, relating to particular instances which, though they may be important, do not amount to continuous control by the party outside Parliament.

What party government does mean lies in some combination of these alternatives, none of which should be dismissed out of hand. What is in dispute is the nature of that combination, but in seeking to identify it we should not look for the political equivalent of an immutable mathematical equation or chemical formula. The nature of party government varies according to the balance of representation in the House of Commons, the attitudes of MPs, the personalities and characters of the Prime Minister and his ministerial colleagues, the actual and perceived role of the party organisations, the attitudes of party supporters and their relationship with the leadership, and, by no means least, the prevailing political, economic and social situation at home and abroad. That Parliament is an integral part of the system of government in Britain there can be no doubt, but, just as it is unrealistic to regard Parliament as a great forum of the nation which determines the affairs of state and decides the fate of governments, it is equally unrealistic to regard Parliament as no more than a cipher. If Parliament is no more than this, then an extraordinary amount of time and effort is devoted to what, by definition, should be a formality. Nor should Parliament be regarded as *the* focal point of national political activity; it is one of several focal points, of which the Prime Minister and the Cabinet is another, and the Whitehall Departments a third. The constitutional powers of Parliament are subject to the constraints of party government: the significance of Parliament, however, lies not in its powers, but in its existence, for we do not have a system of government *by* Parliament, but of government *through* Parliament.

3 Parliament and its functions

The functions of Parliament

In Chapter 2 the basic function of Parliament was defined as examining and questioning government policy and activity (or lack of it). Parliament, however, is a multifunctional institution in that it performs a variety of roles: some contribute to its basic function, some are in addition to it. These functions are summarised in Table 3.1.

With the exception of the judicial function, it can be seen that in each case the House of Commons is more important than the House of Lords in performing the various functions of Parliament. In some cases, such as finance or the recruiting of ministers, the House of Commons is much more important than the Lords; in other areas, such as legislation, importance is more evenly shared. In the case of representation much depends on how the term is defined, especially the House of Lords; this is discussed in the next chapter.

It is also apparent that all the functions are performed by one or other, or both, of the two Houses as a whole, but some may also be performed by individual members of either House. Both Houses, for instance, collectively scrutinise government activity through committees, but it is also open to individuals to carry out the same function by asking parliamentary questions or tabling and signing motions. Similarly, both Houses participate collectively in the legislative role, but backbench MPs and peers may not only propose amendments to bills, but may introduce bills (known as private members' or peers' bills) themselves.

In a political context legitimacy may be defined as the grounds on which political power is exercised in a society and the extent to which the political system is accepted by that society. Political institutions such as Parliament may contribute to that legitimacy by

Table 3.1   The functions of Parliament

| Function | Performed by | | | |
	House of Commons	House of Lords	Collectively	Individually
Legitimising	X	x	x	
Representative	X	x	x	x
Financial	X	x	x	
Redressing of grievances	X	x	x	x
Legislative	X	x	x	x
Recruiting of ministers	X	x	x	
Scrutinising and informing	X	x	x	x
Judicial		X	x†	

* X indicates the more important of the two Houses in performing a particular function, x the less important.
† Performed exclusively by the Law Lords (the up to eleven Lords of Appeal, the Lord Chancellor and any former Lord Chancellors).

being regarded as the proper channel for certain political actions and by conferring an aura of legal and accepted authority on those actions. A group of distinguished and respected lawyers may suggest a change in the law, but, however sensible and acceptable their suggestion may be, unless and until the law has been changed by Parliament it remains nothing more than a suggestion. Equally Parliament may pass a foolish law or a law which has unforeseen consequences, but it remains the law until Parliament sees fit to change or repeal it. The very legitimacy of the government depends on the authority conferred on it by the electorate through Parliament.

Parliament's *legitimising* role could be regarded as the original function of Parliament in that all pre-parliamentary precedents – the meetings of feudal tenants-in-chief in Norman times and the early "parliaments" of de Montfort and Henry III – stemmed primarily from the desire to secure support for the policies of those in power or seeking power; in other words, these early assemblies were called largely to confer legitimacy on the actions of the kings or barons, as the case may be, and to provide them with authority for their future actions. Parliaments could be, and on a number of occasions were, "packed" with the supporters of one faction or another, just as in a later age elections were determined largely by bribery, corruption and patronage, and to that extent the legitimacy that Parliament conferred was a façade behind which political reality operated. Yet the fact that the need for parliamentary legitimacy was felt is important in itself, just as successive monarchs after John felt it desirable to reissue or confirm Magna Carta. The legitimacy that Parliament has conferred and continues to confer is the basis of the rule of law. Governments gratefully accept the moral authority of Parliament which enables them to implement their policies and that it is desirable that those policies should be implemented, as in the Fifth Amendment to the American Constitution, "by due process of law".

The major means by which support was and still is elicited is through *representation*. Early Parliaments varied considerably in their composition, but the historical inequality of representation in the House of Commons need not concern us here. Suffice it to say that Parliament's claim to legitimacy rested largely on its claim to be a body representative of the interests of and drawn territorially from the country as a whole; a claim which is still jealously asserted. The House of Commons regards itself as a body authorised (by virtue of being elected by universal adult suffrage) to discuss national affairs and, where appropriate, determine their course. Moreover, Members of Parliament see themselves as territorial representatives charged with the task of protecting the interests of their constituents. As we shall see, however, the right to interpret the representative role is claimed collectively by the House of Commons and individually by its members, leaving the electorate to judge the efficacy of that representation at elections.

Although early Parliaments were called to secure general support for policies, they were frequently called to legitimise one matter in particular, namely the raising of taxes, from which Parliament's subsequent financial function developed. In due course Parliament acquired the right to approve the purposes to which taxes were put and to examine the national accounts. The right of consent to taxation and to authorise public expenditure still form the basis of parliamentary financial procedure, although as a means of exerting financial control it is largely ineffective. Nonetheless, the government is obliged to present annually to Parliament its proposals for expenditure and taxation, and this provides important opportunities for the House of Commons in particular to fulfil its scrutinising and informing function.

Historically the right of consent to taxation gave Parliament its most important and powerful weapon: the demand for the redress of grievances before the granting of supply, or authority to raise money. Initially this took the form of demands for the redress by the king of particular and limited grievances. That process continues today, both generally and in the form of MPs taking up individual cases with the government or the minister concerned.

Gradually Parliament began to take broader initiatives, seeking remedies to more general matters and eventually establishing a legislative role for itself. Legislation, whether in the form of bills (proposed Acts of Parliament) or statutory instruments (rules and regulations issued by ministers under the authority of an Act of Parliament), must be presented to Parliament and, although it can be argued that for both reasons of time and the extent to which governments can normally control parliamentary business, Parliament's ability to reject or even modify legislation is limited, this again reinforces the scrutinising and informing function.

A natural, though by no means inevitable, development was that Parliament should wish to exert more detailed control over the executive, and this it did through the procedural devices of debate and, later, parliamentary questions and committees. This process was facilitated by the decline in importance of the monarchy and ministers' increasing dependence for office on parliamentary support, which led to the development of the doctrine of ministerial responsibility. A crucial concomitant was that Parliament became the source of ministerial recruitment, and this in the twentieth century became concentrated increasingly on the House of Commons. Although the electorate normally determines which of the party leaders will become Prime Minister, the choice of party leaders lies largely with the MPs of each party. The House of Commons therefore determines the limits of the electorate's choice. If the electorate denies a majority to any party, the choice of Prime Minister and formation of a government reverts to the parties, although their choice is constrained by the results of the election. Thus even if Parliament does not directly choose the Prime Minister, it certainly plays a crucial part.

By convention, the Prime Minister must now come from the Commons, as must most of the ministers he appoints. When first appointed to office most ministers have served several years in Parliament, either as MPs or peers (occasionally as both). Those appointed to Cabinet posts will often have been in Parliament ten or more years and will often have served as junior and middle-ranking ministers. There are exceptions, but they are normally exceptions which prove the general rule that aspiring ministers have served a parliamentary apprenticeship.

Parliament's functions are in practice interdependent, but none more so than the scrutinising and informing function. In spite of its limited influence over finance and legislation Parliament uses its financial and legislative procedures to scrutinise government policies and elicit information about government activities. These procedures, together with the doctrine of ministerial responsibility and the physical presence of ministers in Parliament, force the government to explain and defend its policies publicly. Furthermore, *Hansard*, the verbatim report of Parliament's proceedings, is published daily; the proceedings and reports of parliamentary committees are also published; and the government and various official bodies present to Parliament a large number of documents (reports, accounts, policy proposals, etc.), most of which are also published. Thus an enormous amount of information is available not only to MPs but to the public as well. In addition the activities of Parliament receive a good deal of attention from the press, radio and television, although inevitably this is highly selective in content. Publicity, however, is one of Parliament's most important weapons and, used effectively, publicity (to adapt Dr Johnson's epigram) concentrates a government's mind wonderfully.

The way in which Parliament performs its functions will now be examined by looking in turn at the parliamentary year, the parliamentary day and, in order to complete the perspective, the Member of Parliament's day.

The parliamentary year

The parliamentary year or session normally lasts from October to

October, with breaks or adjournments at Christmas, Easter, Whitsun and in the summer. The House of Commons meets on approximately 170–180 and the House of Lords on approximately 140–150 days a year. The two Houses usually take adjournments at more or less the same time, but whereas the Commons meet every day of the week except Saturday and Sunday, the Lords meet regularly on Tuesday, Wednesday and Thursday, on *most* Mondays, and occasionally on Fridays, and the times of the two Houses differ.

One of the factors which complicates the parliamentary year is that it does not coincide with the official financial year, which runs from the beginning of April in one year to the end of March in the next. Parliamentary financial procedure is easier to understand, however, if several points are appreciated.

First, that Parliament does not *finally* authorise expenditure and taxation until July of each year, three months after the financial year has begun. Although the government presents its main proposals for expenditure (the Estimates) to the House of Commons in February, they do not receive statutory approval until the passing of the Appropriation Act in July. Parliament therefore authorises sufficient funds to cover the period between the end of the financial year and the passing of the Appropriation Act by approving the Civil (that is, all non-military) and Defence Votes on Account. Similarly, the government presents its taxation proposals (contained in the Budget) in late March or early April, but they are not finally approved until the Finance Act is passed in July. In the meantime temporary approval is given to those tax changes which need to have immediate effect, under the Provisional Collection of Taxes Act, 1968.

Second, during each financial year government departments often find that their financial needs outstrip the amounts of money voted to them by Parliament in the previous year; or they may find they need additional money for the forthcoming year after they have already presented their estimates. They therefore submit to the House of Commons supplementary estimates to cover this additional expenditure. The winter and spring Supplementary Estimates cover the current year and the summer Supplementary Estimates cover the forthcoming year. A similar device exists to deal with departmental deficits that may emerge after the financial year has ended; these are known as Excess Votes.

Third, the various items of financial business are incorporated in four separate bills. The Consolidated Fund No. 1 Bill incorporates the winter Supplementary Estimates and the Civil, Defence and House of Commons Votes on Account; the Consolidated Fund No. 2 Bill incorporates the spring Supplementary Estimates and Excess Votes; the Consolidated Fund Bill No. 3, more commonly known as the Appropriation Bill, incorporates the Main Civil and Defence Estimates and the summer Supplementary Estimates; and, as we have already seen, the Budget proposals are incorporated in the Finance Bill.

Finally, only three days are specifically allocated for discussion of the Estimates and the debates on the Consolidated Fund Bills are not strictly confined to the expenditure proposals they contain. Thus the three further days allocated to the Consolidated Fund Bills are by convention used by backbench MPs to raise matters of administration or policy, the only proviso being that such matters must be related to the expenditure for which the bill seeks approval. In a strictly financial sense supply procedure is largely a formality: the Estimates are voted on, but no government has had an estimate reduced by the House of Commons since 1920. Apart from its legal necessity the significance of supply procedure lies in the use to which the time is put: it is the most important source of parliamentary time available to the opposition and provides backbenchers with limited but useful parliamentary time.

The same is not true of the time devoted to the Finance Bill, which is discussed in considerable detail and may be significantly amended, although the government will normally get its way.

A brief explanation of the types of legislation is also helpful in understanding the parliamentary year. Drafts of proposed legislation are presented to Parliament in the form of a bill. When a bill becomes law it is known as an Act of Parliament. Bills may be introduced into either of the two Houses of Parliament by any peer or MP. There are, however, three types of bills. These are, first, public bills, which relate to matters of public policy and usually have general application to the whole nation; second, private bills, which confer particular powers or benefits on a person but more usually nowadays on a body of persons, such as a local authority, a company or a nationalised industry; and third, hybrid bills, which are public bills, parts of which affect private rights. Private bills and hybrid bills are subject to a separate procedure and neither they nor the procedure need concern us here. It should be further noted that public bills may be further divided into government bills and private members' bills which should not be confused with private bills, but are public bills introduced by backbench MPs. The majority of public bills which eventually receive the royal assent are government bills. Furthermore, only a few government bills fail to be passed each session, usually through lack of parliamentary time rather than rejection. The majority of private members' bills fail to pass, sometimes because the government opposes them, sometimes because sufficient backbench support is lacking or opposition too strong, but mainly through lack of time.

All public bills must pass through five stages in each House. The first stage or first reading is a formality: the bill is introduced and the House orders it to be printed. The second reading is a bill's first major hurdle: the House debates the principles of the bill and decides whether it should proceed further.

The third stage is called the committee stage: the bill is either sent to a standing committee of the House, which consists of between sixteen and fifty MPs appointed in proportion to the party divisions in the House, or a committee of the whole House, which, as the term implies, consists of all members sitting as a committee. The significance of this is that, whereas a member may only speak once to a motion in a normal debate, in committee he may speak as often as he can catch the chairman's eye, a procedure which facilitates the detailed discussion of the bill clause by clause, which is the purpose of the committee stage. In the House of Commons most public bills are sent to standing committees, the exceptions being bills of major constitutional importance, short, non-controversial bills of minor importance, bills requiring a very swift passage, and, sometimes, a controversial government bill which, for tactical reasons, the government thinks it can manage better in a committee of the whole. This procedure was followed in the case of Conservative trade union legislation, such as the Industrial Relations Bill in 1971 and the Employment Bill in 1982, for instance. Very occasionally a bill may be referred to a select committee in either House. Unlike the standing committees, select committees can take oral and written evidence from witnesses and have been used for subjects such as obscene publications or military discipline. In addition in recent sessions a few bills have been referred to special standing committees, which may take evidence like select committees and then take the committee stage of the bill in the normal way. However, the government has been reluctant to make widespread use of them. In the House of Lords most bills are dealt with in committee of the whole.

The fourth stage is the report stage, at which the House considers any amendments made in committee. Obviously this stage is usually fairly short if the bill has been taken in a committee of the whole.

The fifth and final stage is the third reading, in which debate is restricted to the contents of the bill, as amended at the committee and report stages, and only verbal amendments (changes of wording designed to clarify the meaning of the bill) are permitted. This does not preclude "blocking" or "reasoned" amendments, but it does prevent the principles of the bill being debated again. As soon as a bill has received its third reading it is sent to the other House. If, for example, amendments to a bill that has already been passed by the Commons are made in the Lords then the bill is returned to the lower house for consideration of the Lords' amendments. These may be accepted or rejected; if they are rejected the Lords may decide not to press their amendments, or there may be negotiations between the two Houses, or the government may decide to apply the provisions of the Parliament Acts and seek to override any disagreement with the Lords, or the bill may simply be lost. Assuming, however, that the bill passes all its stages in both Houses, it then proceeds to the royal assent, ending, as it began, with a formality.

Government proposals for legislation are sometimes presented to Parliament in the form of documents called White Papers, which may be debated before a bill is introduced. Other White Papers are statements of policy or future intentions which do not require legislative action. Each year, for example, the government issues a Defence White Paper, which assesses the current defence situation, and a Public Expenditure White Paper, which outlines plans for government expenditure over the next three years. The government may also present policy proposals to Parliament for discussion in the form of Green Papers.

A new session is normally opened by the Queen at the beginning of November, when the government presents its programme for the year in the Speech from the Throne. The House of Commons then sits for about forty days before rising for the Christmas adjournment. The first few days of the session are devoted to a debate on the Queen's Speech, which takes the form primarily of amendments put down by the official opposition, with counter-amendments from the government side. About half the period before the Christmas recess, however, is devoted to the early stages of bills proposed by the government, to set them along the path to becoming law.

The rest of the period before Christmas is devoted to a variety of matters, some of which are annual occurrences, others varying from year to year. The winter Supplementary Estimates and Civil, Defence and House of Commons Administration Votes on Account are presented to the House of Commons in this period. Other business will vary according to circumstances: the government may wish to have a White Paper debated; government and opposition may agree that a debate on foreign affairs is desirable; the opposition may use one of the nineteen Opposition Days allocated to it to hold a debate on a subject of its choice; the opposition may also put down a motion of censure on the government, for which the government is by convention obliged to find time; and there may be sudden crises, emergencies, unforeseen events which necessitate a debate.

The Christmas adjournment lasts between twenty and thirty days and Parliament resumes its sittings in mid-January. There then follows a period of fifty to sixty days between Christmas and Easter. Legislation occupies about a third of the time and more time is taken up by financial business and other debates. The winter Supplementary Estimates and the Civil, Defence and House of Commons Administration Votes on Account, which were introduced in the House of Commons in November or December, are authorised in January or February by the passing of the Consolidated Fund No. 1 Bill. The spring Supplementary Estimates, Excess Votes for the previous financial year and the Defence Vote of Account are introduced in February or March. These last items are authorised by the passing of the Consolidated Fund No. 2 Bill. The summer Supplementary Estimates and the Main Civil and Defence Estimates are also introduced in March. More government bills are introduced and bills already introduced are taken through their later stages. There is also a debate on defence based on the annual Defence White Paper and there will be debates on other matters on the same lines as described earlier. The Easter adjournment is usually quite short, about ten days or so, and may or may not be preceded by the Budget, depending when Easter falls.

Assuming, for the purposes of this outline of the parliamentary year, that the Budget is presented by the Chancellor of the Exchequer immediately after the Easter adjournment, there then follows a period of about sixty to seventy sitting days, interrupted by another short adjournment for Whitsun of about ten days, which takes Parliament up to the beginning of the summer adjournment towards the end of July. Financial business dominates this period, which is best considered as a whole: the Main Civil and Defence Estimates and the summer Supplementary Estimates have to be authorised by the passing of the Appropriation Bill. The Budget proposals have to be implemented by the passing of the Finance Bill, and this accounts for about two-thirds of the time.

In the meantime the bills introduced earlier in the session will, in some cases, have passed all their stages in the two Houses and have received the royal assent, but others (especially some of the larger and the more controversial ones) will still be in the later stages of the legislative process, and legislation tends to pile up at the end of the session. Sometimes one or two bills are "lost" because if any bill fails to pass all its stages in one session it cannot be taken up in the next session at the stage it had previously reached, but must go through all its stages again. In order to avoid losing legislation in this way Parliament normally meets for a few days in October or early November to deal with any outstanding business before the session is brought to a close. Parliament's main business is normally concluded in July, and there then follows the long summer adjournment, lasting about eighty days. The new session begins almost immediately after the short "tidying-up" period in October.

Although Parliament follows the same basic pattern each year, unless a session is brought to a premature end by a dissolution of Parliament, it is open to the government to vary the number of sitting days and the dates of adjournments. In addition, when Parliament is adjourned it may be recalled for emergency sessions to discuss any urgent matter that might arise. This happened in January 1974 when Parliament was recalled to discuss the energy crisis caused by the reduction in oil supplies by Arab producers and the effect on coal supplies of an overtime ban by miners. Indeed, in 1982 Parliament was recalled twice within the space of twelve days to discuss the invasion of the Falklands by Argentina. On rare occasions Parliament holds emergency sittings on a Saturday. This occurred during the Second World War and, most recently, in 1982 for one of the two emergency debates on the Falklands.

We have already noted that the House of Lords meets less often than the House of Commons and that the periods of adjournment may differ marginally according to the business before each House. Sometimes, for instance, the Lords will sit a week longer than the Commons in the summer in order to deal with legislation already passed by the Commons. More important, however, there are differences in the distribution of business in the two Houses. Because of the financial primacy of the Commons the Lords spend little time on financial business, although they may debate the Defence Estimates and always discuss the Finance Bill. The House of Lords divides its time principally between general debate and dealing with legislation. Because of the virtual absence of financial business there are fewer matters which the Lords are *obliged* to debate and they can therefore range more widely in what they discuss than the Commons.

The House of Lords also plays a distinctive legislative role. Most of the time it spends on legislation is in dealing with bills (mostly government bills) already passed by the Commons. The pressure on time in the latter is such that bills are often inadequately discussed and may have been subject to an agreed or imposed timetable. The government may also have had second thoughts about some of the details of a bill and these can be incorporated during its passage through the Lords. Outside interests have an opportunity to make representations for the amendment of the bill. Finally, although the non-judicial members of the upper House do not participate in its judicial proceedings, the judicial members can make useful contributions to debates, especially on the legal niceties of legislation.

Because of the political primacy of the House of Commons most major government legislation is introduced in the lower House, but non-controversial government legislation is often introduced in the House of Lords. This practice helps to spread Parliament's legislative load more evenly over the session by allowing both Houses to start bills on the legislative path early in the session, and saves the Commons time because bills introduced in the Lords often require little amendment by the lower House. In recent sessions 30 to 40 per cent of government bills were introduced in the House of Lords.

The House of Lords also performs a useful function of a similar kind by introducing bills, known as Consolidation Bills, which bring together in a single statute the various laws regarding a particular matter. In recent sessions the number of Consolidation Bills has ranged from eight to seventeen.

The upper House provides one other useful legislative service to the House of Commons by assuming the greater part of the burden of private legislation. Between thirty and forty private bills are passed each year and about half of these are dealt with first by the Lords. Such bills may, for example, give a local authority the power to construct a local airport, or an oil company to lay a pipeline across private land. The Lords save the Commons time by dealing with the more time-consuming private bills.

While it would be misleading to describe the House of Lords as the legislative assistant of the House of Commons, not only is the Commons politically more important, but it sets the *pace* of the parliamentary year. The Commons would probably pass fewer bills, and certainly less adequately drafted bills, were it not for the help of the Lords, but ultimately which bills and how many bills become law depends on the Commons. The party battle is fought primarily in the House of Commons: the government's principal weapon is normally its majority; the opposition's principal weapon is time.

The time of the House of Commons is distributed between various types of business and between the government, the official opposition and private members or backbenchers. This distribution, especially between types of business, can vary from session to session. More than half the Commons' time is spent dealing with legislation, about a third is taken up by financial business, and the remainder with various other debates, excluding the time devoted to formal business (which is minimal), private business (normally very little) and parliamentary questions. The latter occupy between forty-five and fifty minutes every sitting day except Friday. It should, of course, be borne in mind that much of the time technically spent on financial business is usually devoted to wider issues.

The average number of public bills passed in the eight normal-length sessions between 1971–72 and 1981–82 was sixty-eight, ranging from fifty-one in 1977–78 to eighty-eight in 1975–76. Almost all government bills are passed: 98.3 per cent and 97.9 per cent in 1980–81 and 1981–82 respectively are typical of the success rate; in fact, in

Table 3.2   The distribution of parliamentary time in the House of Commons between the government, the official opposition and backbenchers

	Days	%
Government time	101	57.7
Time conceded by the government	10	5.7
Official opposition time	36	20.6
Private members' time	28	16.0
Total	175	100.0

1979–80 the government managed to secure the passage of every one of its seventy-one bills. Even during periods of minority government, the government gets most of its legislation through. Thus in 1976–77 84.0 per cent of the minority Labour Government's bills were passed, rising to 96.1 per cent in 1977–78, when the government benefited from Liberal support resulting from the Lib-Lab Pact. Compared with this the success rate of private members' and private peers' bills is very low indeed: about a hundred such bills are introduced each year, but even in a good year the success rate will not reach 20 per cent. The main reason can be summed up in a single word: time. The typical distribution of time is shown in Table 3.2.

After deducting the time allocated to private members, and the official opposition, and the time the government must make available for emergency debates and matters for which it is politically expedient to provide time, the government is left with between half and three-fifths of the available time to devote to its business, including some of its essential financial business. However, the amount of time available for government business tends to underestimate the extent to which the government normally controls the business of the House of Commons, and a number of factors need to be taken into account.

1. Private members' time is not inviolable: most of it can be commandeered by the government (this happened between 1945 and 1950), although it is probable that no government would today wish to risk the obloquy that the almost total usurpation of private members' time would entail. Nonetheless, the government still decides which Fridays (the traditional private members'

day) will be devoted to private members' business, how many will be devoted to their bills and how many to their motions. In recent sessions private members' business has had precedence on twenty-one Fridays, twelve for bills and nine for motions. In addition, on four other days motions tabled by backbenchers may be debated until 7 p.m.

2. No private member's bill which is opposed by the government will normally succeed, whilst determined backbench opposition to any bill is usually enough to kill it, unless the government is willing to assist its passage by providing some government time. This occurred during the 1966–70 Parliament, when private members' bills to reform the law on abortion and on divorce were passed with the help of government time.

3. Private members' time is fragmented and cannot be freely used by backbenchers for any purpose they wish. Fridays are divided between bills and motions; the daily half-hour adjournment debates (we deal with these later) and the debates on the Consolidated Fund Bills cannot be used for private members' bills. Although a certain amount can be achieved by procedural ingenuity, the procedural balance lies against backbenchers, especially as they are competing with one another for a limited amount of parliamentary time.

4. Although the amount of time allocated to the official opposition might, at more than one fifth, seem generous, there are practical limitations on its usefulness. There is no means other than that open to private members by which the opposition can introduce its own bills and, given a government majority, they would serve only a propaganda function. Opposition time cannot be used to obstruct the government's legislative programme and, although the opposition chooses the subject for debate, it cannot arbitrarily decide when the debate will take place. That decision is made by the government, although it is a foolish government which does not seek the cooperation of the opposition in the allocation of Opposition Days. The opposition can force a debate by putting down a motion of censure on the government, for which the government must by convention find time, but too frequent use of this device lessens its impact. Thus there are not usually more than one or two censure debates a year.

5. If the government finds that its programme is falling behind

schedule it has several additional weapons in its armoury. Apart from Fridays, the Commons normally adjourns or ends its sittings at 10.30 p.m., but the government can extend the sitting indefinitely, although if the House is still sitting at the time it is due to meet the next day that day's business is lost. In 1980–81 and 1981–82 late night sittings added the equivalent of thirty-seven and thirty-six days respectively to the parliamentary year. The government can also impose a timetable on legislation by which votes on a stage of a bill or discussion of some part of it will take place at a predetermined time, after which the House will go on to the next stage or next part of the bill. If all this is of no avail then the government can extend the session, a far from popular recourse.

6. The government sets the agenda for the House. Each Thursday the Leader of the House of Commons announces the business to be taken the following week. He may, for instance, announce that on Monday the report stage and third reading of a non-controversial government bill will be taken, followed by a debate on a report from a select committee; Tuesday and Wednesday will be devoted to a major two-day debate on the government's economic policy; and on Thursday the second reading of a major government bill will be taken. The opposition may demand that two days be given to the second reading of a major bill or that time be made available for a statement from a particular minister, while individual backbenchers may plead for a debate on this matter or that. The Leader of the House will listen, promise to consult his colleagues, and occasionally accede to a request, but the decision rests with the government.

Of course, much, though not all, of the government's control of the business of the House depends on its having majority support, but even a minority government retains the power of initiative and the precedence accorded to government business in the parliamentary timetable. Certainly when the government does have a majority parliamentary business is conducted very much in the knowledge that the government can use its majority to get its way. The opposition therefore refrains from forcing the government to use its majority at every turn. Such tactics would make life intolerable for both opposition and government, quite apart from inviting similar treatment if and when their roles of government and opposition are reversed. There is, in fact, a considerable amount of cooperation between the two over the handling of parliamentary business, not only in allocating time (the opposition, for example, will quite often cooperate in applying a timetable to legislation and other business), but also in necessitating the attendance of their respective supporters. The demands on MPs' time are often considerable, so demands for attendance vary according to the importance placed by government or opposition on each item of business. The most important business is accorded a three-line whip (the request to attend being underlined three times) and MPs should attend to vote unless illness intervenes or some previous engagement has been accepted with the agreement of the party's whips or managers. A two-line or one-line whip indicates less importance and members may secure pairs, by which government and opposition MPs agree not to vote and so cancel out each other's votes. Such arrangements, however, must be made through the party whips.

It is thus misleading to regard the parliamentary year as totally subject to the tyranny of the government majority. Considerable as the government's control of parliamentary business is, it also depends on, and is therefore constrained by, the practical necessity of co-operation, especially between government and opposition. It is not politic for the government constantly to browbeat the opposition with its majority, nor for the opposition to indulge in frequent and regular obstruction.

The parliamentary day

This and the following section will concentrate on the House of Commons, referring only to the House of Lords where appropriate. Moreover it is not intended to be an exhaustive description of every type of business that can come before the House of Commons.

On every day except Fridays the House of Commons meets at 2.30 p.m. and adjourns at 10.30 p.m., a normal sitting of eight hours. On Fridays the House meets at 9.30 a.m. and adjourns at 3.00 p.m., a normal sitting of five-and-a-half hours. Apart from the fact that the majority of Fridays are devoted to private members' business, the main difference between Fridays and other sitting days is that there is no Question Time on the former.

On some days standing and select committees of the House of

Commons meet in the mornings. Standing committees deal with the committee stage of bills; select committees, which unlike standing committees have the power to take written evidence and hear witnesses, are mostly concerned with conducting investigations into various governmental activities. The meetings of these committees can also take place during the afternoon and evening, when the House is sitting; they are normally attended only by the MPs nominated as members, although all standing committees and most select committees meet in public and other MPs can attend.

The House of Commons is presided over by the Speaker, who is elected from the members of the House at the beginning of each Parliament. Once elected the Speaker cuts all party ties and endeavours to enforce procedure with strict impartiality. Since it is unreasonable to expect the Speaker to preside continuously he is assisted by a Deputy Speaker, officially known as the Chairman of Ways and Means (which was formerly one of the two financial committees of the whole House), and two Deputy Chairmen. When the House sits as a committee of the whole, in fact, the Deputy Speaker or one of the Deputy Chairmen always presides.

Each sitting is opened with prayers by the Speaker's Chaplain. The first business consists of various formal items, such as the announcement by the Speaker of the death of a member, or the moving of a motion for the writ for a by-election by the chief whip of one of the parties (usually a formality). This is followed by private business, mainly consideration of private bills, but discussion of any private business that is opposed is postponed to another day, or sometimes later the same day. Public petitions are also presented at this time by MPs on behalf of the signatories. Nowadays petitions are little more than a hopeful means of securing publicity, and only a handful are presented each year. Altogether the business mentioned so far does not usually take more than five minutes.

The first major piece of business is Question Time, when ministers give oral answers to questions previously submitted in writing by MPs. Far more questions are asked than can be answered in the time available. Each minister is therefore placed on a rota and the questions for a particular minister are grouped together on the Order Paper or agenda. The nearer a minister is to the top of the rota the more likely he is actually to answer questions orally in the House, but questions to those at or near the bottom are unlikely to be reached before the end of Question Time. The Prime Minister always answers questions in the House between 3.15 p.m. and 3.30 p.m. on Tuesdays and Thursdays. In this way MPs get a reasonable chance of directly questioning all ministers in due course. In order to prevent one or more MPs from usurping the whole of Question Time each member is limited to two questions for oral answer per day, of which only one may be addressed to any one minister, and eight questions within ten sitting days; there is also a maximum notice of ten sitting days. Immediately after a minister has given his answer to a parliamentary question any member present (though it is often the member who tabled the original question) may ask one or more supplementary questions. The number and extent of these follow-up questions is at the discretion of the Speaker, but in no circumstances will the Speaker allow a debate to develop out of supplementary questions. Any questions which do not receive an oral answer will receive a written answer in *Hansard*, unless the member concerned asks that the question be put down for oral answer at a later date. About a hundred questions a day are put down for oral answer, but not more than thirty will normally be answered in the House. Far more questions are given written replies, including not only those which do not receive an oral answer, but those to which the member has requested a written answer. There is no limit to the number of questions for written answer which a member may ask and they provide a very useful method of extracting information from ministers.

Question Time ends at 3.30 p.m. and may be followed by a further type of parliamentary question called a private notice question, by which an urgent question, too late to meet the minimum forty-eight hours notice required for ordinary questions, can be asked. The Speaker decides whether the matter is sufficiently urgent to merit a private notice question. In practice this is a method sometimes used by ministers to make announcements on policy or other matters by having a private notice question asked by a government supporter. It is also the traditional method by which the Leader of the Opposition asks questions. In general, however, parliamentary questions are the preserve of backbenchers. Apart from the weekly announcement by the Leader of the House of the business to be taken the following week, which is made in response to a private notice question, about two private notice questions are answered each week.

It is not always possible for ministerial announcements to be made under the auspices of private notice questions and ministerial statements can therefore be made immediately after private notice questions. It is possible for MPs to question the minister about his statement, but, again no debate is allowed to develop.

Casual vacancies in the membership of the House of Commons are filled at by-elections and it is at this point that new MPs are introduced into the House of Commons, flanked by two sponsors, who are usually MPs of the same party as the new member. Following the introduction of any new members there is the opportunity for any MP to move that an emergency debate should take place under Standing Order 10 "for the purpose of discussing a specific and important matter that should have urgent consideration". The Speaker rules whether the matter comes within the terms of Standing Order 10 and, if he rules that it does, the House decides whether it will be debated. If the House does decide to hold a debate it will normally be held at 7 p.m. the following day, although if it is regarded as very urgent or occurs on a Thursday, it is held at 7 p.m. the same day. One or two such debates a year are held.

Various other items of business are now taken, such as personal statements by ministers who have resigned from the government explaining why they have done so, or by a member who wishes to correct a report about him that may have appeared in the press; or a member may wish to complain that a breach of parliamentary privilege has occurred. Most complaints of breach of privilege involve allegations that someone has cast aspersions on the House or on individual MPs. A newspaper report may have suggested that a member has acted corruptly, for instance. The Speaker rules whether a *prima facie* breach of privilege has occurred and if he does then the matter is referred to the Committee of Privileges, which consists of a number of senior MPs. The Committee investigates and reports back to the House. If the House finds that a breach of privilege has occurred the offender will normally be reprimanded (in times past offenders were sometimes committed to prison). An MP who is found guilty of a breach of privilege may suffer the penalty of being expelled from the House of Commons. Such cases are not very common, although MPs tend to be sensitive about parliamentary privilege and allegations of breaches are fairly common.

In spite of the great variety of business that can occur at this stage in the parliamentary day, it is normally disposed of by 3.45 p.m., little more than an hour after the sitting has begun, including, of course, the time devoted to questions for oral answer. This is partly because most of these items are not daily occurrences and partly because the House deliberately disposes of them quickly.

The daily business of the House of Commons is divided into two unequal parts, the first of which has now been described. The second part is known as "public business", when the Commons deals with the various stages of bills, its financial business and holds its setpiece debates. There are, however a few items of business that are taken "at the commencement of public business" because they relate to public business but are not part of the main business to be dealt with that day. These include the presentation of bills for first reading, when the bill is ordered to be printed and the date for its second reading is set; motions put down by the government relating to the business of the House; and the formal nomination of members of select committees of the House of Commons. Under the second item the government may move a motion to alter the order of business on the Order Paper, or to give government business precedence in time normally allocated to private members, or to provide for a morning sitting of the House. It is also at this point that a backbench MP may seek to introduce a private member's bill under the "ten-minute rule". On Tuesdays and Wednesdays, following prior notice, a member may introduce a bill and speak for ten minutes in support of it. An opposing speech, also of ten minutes, may be made and the House decides whether leave to introduce the bill is granted. If it is the bill must take its place in the queue of private members' bills and its chances of reaching the statute book are not very great. Moreover, only one such bill may be introduced on each occasion. Nonetheless, it does provide an opportunity for backbenchers to suggest legislation and from time to time ten-minute rule bills do become law.

Matters taken "at the commencement of public business" do not usually occupy more than fifteen minutes or so and mark the watershed of the parliamentary day. All but half-an-hour of the rest of the parliamentary day is normally devoted to the main business set down in the Order Paper. It may consist of one item of business, such as the second reading debate of a bill or a one-day debate on foreign affairs, or it may be one of the opposition's allotted days, or it may consist of several items, such as the report of a select committee, a short debate on some government policy, short debates on non-controversial bills, and many items which may not be debated at all because no one wishes to debate or oppose them. The latter can, of course, apply to any of the substantive stages of a bill.

Business may be interrupted at 7 p.m. to hold an emergency debate under Standing Order 10, or to deal with opposed private business, as described earlier. But this is unusual and the House of Commons usually continues to deal with its main business until at least 10 p.m. After the main business has been dealt with, seldom before 10 p.m., the House deals with statutory instruments that have been laid before Parliament. These, as mentioned earlier, are regulations issued by ministers under the authority of an Act of Parliament. Not all statutory instruments have to be laid before Parliament, but those that do may require confirmation before becoming effective, or may be rejected within a specified period of time, or may simply be presented to Parliament for information. It is those coming under the first two categories that are dealt with after the main business and discussion on them is normally limited under standing orders.

At 10 p.m. the debate in progress either comes to an end or is interrupted to enable the government to move a motion that the "ten o'clock rule" be suspended, which means that the House will then sit beyond the normal hour of adjournment and have a late night sitting. Whichever happens, the parliamentary day is brought to an end by a half-hour debate called the adjournment debate. The adjournment debate is private members' time and each day a backbencher has the opportunity to raise a matter of his choice and have it debated for half-an-hour. MPs ballot for the opportunity to move the adjournment motion (except for one day when the Speaker chooses a member whose subject he thinks merits debate) and a minister replies to the debate. Understandably the adjournment debate is a much-prized period and provides an effective opportunity for backbenchers to make an individual contribution to the parliamentary day.

The member of Parliament's day
There is no such creature as the average member of Parliament and therefore no such phenomenon as the average member's day. Of course, MPs do have certain things in common. Each MP receives a salary of £16,904 (1985 – rising to £18,500 by 1987) a year, a secretarial

allowance of £12,000, free postage and telephone calls on parliamentary business, certain travel allowances, a subsistence allowance to help support him in London when Parliament is sitting, and, provided he has served as a member for at least four years and is sixty or over, he will receive a parliamentary pension on retirement. He will also, if he wishes, either have a room or "desk space" in or near the Palace of Westminster, make use of the facilities provided by the House of Commons Library, obtain meals and other refreshments in the Palace, seek the advice of the various officials of the House, especially the Clerks (who will advise him on parliamentary procedure), and enjoy what Dickens once described as "the best club in London".

A major factor distinguishing one member from another is the constituency each represents. Some represent urban, some rural constituencies. Some constituencies are replete with social problems: slums, declining industries, overstretched social services, poor communications and so on; others lie in prosperous and economically expanding areas; some have elements of both. The nature of his constituency is likely to play an important part in determining an MP's attitude towards his work as a constituency representative, in particular the extent to which he sees himself fulfilling a welfare officer role for his constituents. Most MPs hold regular "surgeries" to which constituents can bring their problems and discuss them personally with their member. In urban seats these can usually be held in one place, but in rural areas the MP may hold surgeries in different parts of the constituency. Some MPs have their homes in or near their constituencies and have a flat or house in London, or live in lodgings or a hotel when the House is sitting; others live in or near London and visit or have a second residence in their constituencies; a few maintain more than two residences; what most have in common is that they spend some time, often quite a lot of time, in their constituencies. For MPs with constituencies in or near London constituency work can sometimes be fitted in in the evening as well as at weekends, but for most MPs it is weekend work, catching a train (or possibly a plane for those with more distant constituencies) late on Thursday or Friday, returning overnight on Sunday or on Monday, according to the parliamentary business.

Quite apart from parliamentary business and constituency work there may be other calls on an MP's time. Up to ninety-one members may hold ministerial posts, for which they are paid salaries ranging from £66,250 (1985) for the Lord Chancellor, who receives an additional salary as Speaker of the House of Lords, and £53,600 (1985) for the Prime Minister (although the present Lord Chancellor and Prime Minister decline to draw their full salaries), to £25,310 for a government whip. Ministerial duties are very time-consuming and, apart from those occasions when they must be in the House of Commons to deal with the parliamentary business of their Departments, ministers normally spend at least their mornings on departmental work. This is one of the major reasons why Parliament does not have more "civilised" working hours. Ministers aside, a study conducted on behalf of the Review Body on Top Salaries (the Plowden Committee). which makes recommendations on MPs' salaries and allowances, found that 72 per cent of all backbenchers had part-time occupations outside Parliament, leaving 28 per cent who could be regarded as full-time Members of Parliament. The amount of time spent on these outside occupations varied from 32 per cent who spent less than five hours on outside work when Parliament was sitting to 3 per cent who spent thirty or more hours per week.[1] The working hours of Parliament do facilitate the pursuit of outside occupations by MPs and it is not quite akin to the "moonlighting" associated with some other jobs. Indeed, some members argue that this outside work enhances their value as MPs by keeping them in touch with the "real world"; it also enhances their incomes which for many was a necessity before the salary increase and improved allowances introduced in 1972.

One of the effects outside work has on the working of the House of Commons is that a significant proportion of important but routine work is undertaken by two hundred parliamentary "work-horses" the two hundred or so full-time or nearly full-time MPs. It is these MPs who mostly man the standing committees dealing with the committee stage of bills and, to a lesser extent, who man the select committees scrutinising a wide range of government activities. This is not to say that other MPs who spend less time on their parliamentary duties do not make a valuable contribution – that cannot be measured in time alone; nor is it necessarily to argue that all MPs should be full-time, although the trend is towards more full-time members. A better perspective is achieved if another statistic from the Plowden Report is quoted: only 3 per cent of backbenchers claimed to spend less than forty-one hours per week on parliamentary business while the House is sitting compared with 8 per cent who claimed to spend over ninety-one hours; the average was sixty-seven hours. The term "parliamentary business" in this context included not only time in the House, whether on the floor or in committee, but time spent on constituency work, preparation for debates and committee work, attending party meetings, and so on. Bearing in mind that including committee work the House of Commons meets for about forty-eight hours per week, an average of sixty-seven hours spent on parliamentary work is quite high. Of course, this is only when the House is sitting and MPs do have much more time during adjournments, but the needs and demands of constituents do not disappear and politics does not stop merely because Parliament is not sitting. Indeed, the Plowden survey found that the average time spent by backbenchers on parliamentary business when the House was not sitting was forty hours per week.[2]

It is also important to appreciate that the majority of MPs specialise in their parliamentary work by concentrating largely on those areas in which they can claim experience, expertise, knowledge or merely interest and, of course, invariably on those areas which are important to their constituencies. In some cases the two go together and a member with experience in a particular industry will sit for a constituency in which that industry is important. This is sometimes the case with Labour MPs financially supported (or sponsored) by trade unions, but specialisation stems primarily from the interests and experience of the member himself and is reflected in his parliamentary activity. Moreover, he will usually pursue these interests by being a member of the relevant party subject committees of MPs which meet regularly at Westminster to discuss party policies, and he may also be a member of one or more of the various inter-party bodies, such as the Anglo-German Group, the Chemical Industry Group, the United Nations Group, or the Road Safety Group.

A member's interests play an important part in determining which debates he attends, which committees he sits on, and so on and therefore how his parliamentary activity will vary from day to day. This remains true even if the MP receives a three-line whip requiring him to vote in one or more divisions on a particular day: attendance at debates is not a prerequisite of voting in divisions and the division bells summon members not only from the Chamber of the House of Commons, but from all over the Palace of Westminster and its environs. Regardless of his special interests, of course, a member will often attend major debates, sometimes because the subject is of more general interest, sometimes because the parties' "big guns" are in action, and often because it is of major political importance. Members can find out what is being discussed in the House and who is speaking by means of the closed circuit television receivers located in various parts of the Palace; the sound of the gong on the television receiver announcing a change of speaker (and from time to time subject) may create a flurry of activity as MPs hurry to the Chamber, or the response may be no more than a cursory glance at the receiver.

The extent to which a member may have special interests and the extent to which he pursues them is likely to affect his attitude towards his role as an MP, but this is an issue which goes far beyond the question of specialisation. We have, in fact, almost come full circle, having started by discussing the functions of Parliament and coming now to the functions of the individual MP. This is a complex matter over which there is a good deal of argument and we have already said something about three elements of it: the constituency role, whether MPs should be full-time or part-time, and the extent to which they specialise. Cutting across these is a more fundamental argument over the role of Parliament and how that role may best be fulfilled. It is primarily an argument over whether Parliament can best fulfil its principal function of scrutinising the executive through investigatory committees or by means of debates in the House of Commons, a question we examine in more detail in Chapter 5. In part this can be linked with the full-time/part-time syndrome in that full-time or nearly full-time MPs are more likely to favour the use of committees, and it is they who largely man them, but the correlation is by no means absolute. Similarly, interests in certain areas lead MPs to favour committees, whereas interests in others lead them to believe that the Chamber is a more effective arena for their pursuit. Again, most MPs recognise and accept a constituency role, but some strongly resent the extent to which they are expected to act as constituency welfare officers. Further differences emerge in the area of services and facilities: some MPs welcome the decision to provide every member with a room and feel that they should have extensive research and information services and staff paid for entirely from public funds, but others feel that the provision of rooms for MPs and of more services and facilities has undermined the club atmosphere of the House and is destroying the intimacy of its political life. These differences should be borne in mind when considering the member's day.

The Plowden survey also found that 69 per cent of backbench MPs had the assistance of one or more full-time staff and the rest had one or more part-time staff. The same survey found that 60 per cent of backbench MPs had research assistants.[3]

Most members probably start the day by dealing with their post, either personally or with the help of their secretaries. Either then or later in the day the member will dictate replies to letters, taking up constituency cases with ministers, local authorities, and so on. It is difficult to generalise about the amount of post an MP receives, since not only does this vary considerably from one member to another, but can vary markedly over time. In broad terms it can be divided into at least seven categories: personal or semipersonal correspondence asking the MP to attend a luncheon or dinner, address some organisation, open a fete or bazaar, and the like; letters from constituents asking the MP to deal with some grievance; letters from non-constituents raising grievances with which the MP has become identified in the public mind; letters from various individuals, constituents and non-constituents alike, expressing their point of view on this or that policy, which again are often influenced by the known interests and views of the member; letters from various organisations seeking the member's support for various policies, some of which amount to little more than circulars sent to all or a large number of MPs, others being more carefully tailored and distributed to maximise their impact; circulars proper from all manner of organisations, most of which have little or no impact on MPs and suffer a swift demise in the wastepaper basket; and letters from cranks, ranging from those which warn of society's impending doom to those which are abusive. Taking all categories together a survey of MPs in 1967 found that most members received somewhere between seventy-five and two hundred letters a week.[4] There can be little doubt that these figures have increased substantially since then: pressure group activity has increased considerably and in 1983 one Conservative MP claimed that he received an average of seventy-five letters per week from constituents alone.

Receiving letters is something all MPs have in common, even if the number does vary considerably, but beyond this point the member's day can also vary, both from day to day and between members. If the MP is currently a member of a standing or select committee then it may be meeting in the morning, usually beginning at 10.30. If he is not on any committees he may spend the morning on other parliamentary work, such as preparing a speech, dealing with constituency cases, taking a delegation to meet a minister, meeting a constituent or representative of a pressure group, attending a party committee, and so on, but he may be one of those members with an occupation outside Parliament and the mornings provide an ideal time to pursue such interests.

The member may lunch with colleagues, which will perhaps provide a chance of pursuing a mutual interest such as a private member's bill currently before the House, or he may have been invited to address a gathering of businessmen at lunch. After lunch the member may have arranged to meet some constituents who have asked for tickets for the Strangers' (or public) Gallery of the House of Commons. He will meet them in the Central Lobby shortly before the House meets at 2.30 p.m. and, after watching the Speaker's Procession cross the Lobby and proceed into the House, he will see them safely ensconced in the gallery. Later in the afternoon he may take them for tea in the Strangers' Cafeteria or, if it is summer, on the terrace overlooking the river.

Whether he must meet constituents or not, it is likely that the member will want to attend Question Time (and he must if he has a question for oral answer on the Order Paper), but once questions and the other miscellaneous items which follow are over, the member in company with the great majority will probably leave the Chamber, unless the debate is of great interest in terms of subject or frontbench speakers or both, or, of course, he himself hopes to speak. If he does hope to speak he will normally have informed the Speaker, who tries to fit in any as many MPs as possible bearing in mind the need to secure a balanced debate, and it is normal practice for the member to attend at least part of the debate before and after speaking.

In the meantime some other constituents may have arrived in the Central Lobby and one of the uniformed attendants may be looking for the member with a "Green Card" which gives the name of the person wishing to see the member and briefly states his business. A quarter of an hour may now be spent listening to a complaint against a landlord or a request for help in securing some social security benefits. A number of MPs may also find that they are being lobbied by members of a pressure group – teachers, miners, or taxi-drivers. London MPs and those representing seats near London are more likely to have visits from constituents, and this may create a greater burden on them compared with their colleagues sitting for more distant constituencies. On the other hand a constituent from Yorkshire or Scotland may expect rather more attention from his MP than one who is able to get to Westminster more easily, though the logic of this does not always prevail.

The afternoon and early evening may afford opportunities to attend meetings in or near London if the member does not wish to attend the debate, although there may be some committee meeting during this time of the day. If there is an emergency debate the member may want to be present at 7 p.m. when it begins, and this may mean cancelling engagements for the rest of the evening. When the House is dealing with the committee or report stage of a bill there may be a whole series of divisions and, even though the member may not be in the Chamber, he will normally remain within earshot of the division bells. He can, of course, work in the Library, chat to colleagues or use one of the television rooms; or he may be interested in the bill concerned and stay in the Chamber.

At 10 p.m. (or later if a late sitting has been agreed) the House will begin the half-hour adjournment debate. This does not usually attract more than a handful of MPs, including the minister who attends to reply to the matter raised by the member moving the adjournment. Adjournment debates are usually quiet and almost conversational, bringing to an end what may have been a day of fierce political battles, punctuated with cheers and countercheers, invective and high feeling, and almost certainly exhausting.

Attempts to assess parliamentary activity in terms of attendance at the House (of which there is no official record) and even more so by how often a member speaks in a debate are very misleading. The parliamentary day does not lend itself to this sort of analysis and nor does the member's day.

Parliament and procedure

It is sometimes said that Parliament indulges in too much unnecessary ceremonial and has too many time-wasting procedures, but such criticisms should not be extended to condemn procedure itself.

Whatever faults may be detected in the procedures of Parliament they do not obviate the fact that procedure is the necessary framework without which Parliament would break down. Parliamentary procedure is elaborate because the business of Parliament is complex and because some sort of balance must be achieved between the need to expedite that business and the need to subject it to effective scrutiny. Where that balance should lie is a matter of opinion, but in the absence of rules it would not exist.

4 Parliament and representation

Parliament and its functions 53

The meaning of representation

Parliamentary government is a major form of representative government in that through the House of Commons representatives of the people share in the governmental process. We have already looked at some aspects of what "sharing in the governmental process" means and will return to this later, but our concern now is with the concept of representation.

A.H. Birch has pointed out that the term "representative" is generally used in one of three ways:

> In the first place, the term is used to denote an agent or delegate, a person whose function is to protect and if possible advance the interests of the individual or group on whose behalf he is acting. . . .
>
> In the second place, the term is commonly used to describe persons and assemblies who have been freely elected: in this usage the characteristic of a representative would seem to be the manner of his selection rather than his behaviour. . . .
>
> There is a third usage of the term which is different again, and is also very common. In this usage the term signifies that a person is or group of people are typical of a class.[1]

Used in the first way the term can be applied to an ambassador, a barrister or the spokesman for an organisation. With varying degrees of freedom representatives in this sense are acting under instructions. Politically the significance of this usage is concerned with the extent to which a representative may be regarded as a delegate subject to instructions from the body he represents. For example, the representatives sent by constituency Labour Parties, trade unions and other organisations affiliated to the Labour Party to the annual Party conference are called delegates. Some of the matters to be dealt with at the conference may have been discussed by the local party or at trade union conferences, and the delegates concerned may have been given instructions to vote for or against particular resolutions. In other cases matters may not have been discussed and the delegate is left to decide whether to support or oppose particular resolutions. Delegates are also usually given discretion to deal with matters in the light of circumstances, such as proposed amendments to resolutions, concessions from the platform, or the impact of speeches in the debate.

In a sense, when political parties seek or claim a mandate from the people at the time of a general election they are seeking or claiming instructions from the people. They may seek or claim either a general instruction to govern or specific approval of particular measures, but quite often both. Such mandates may be dismissed as political rhetoric or regarded as the justification for the exercise of power and in Chapter 6 we consider the mandate as an expression of public opinion.

The second use of the term "representative" refers to the means by which representatives are chosen, and in a political context this means by election. It is usually argued that the term "representative" is only appropriate where the elector is offered a genuine choice. That choice must involve either the freedom to choose between two or more candidates, or, if there is only one candidate standing, the freedom to reject that candidate. It is also assumed that elections are not determined by bribery, corruption or some other means of manipulation. Unfortunately there are many fairly subtle means of manipulation, such as skilful use of the mass media, which are not usually illegal and are often difficult to make illegal or to control. Thus in theory a representative assembly is a body whose members have been elected rather than nominated or appointed, but in practice they may or may not have been freely elected, and what constitutes a "free" election is ultimately a matter of opinion. For example, if, by skilful use of the mass media, a party projects an attractive but false image of its leader and wins the election as a result, is it a free election? We may ask whether the fact that the Conservative and Labour Parties are financially better off than the Liberal and Social Democratic Parties, which gives them an important advantage in the production of election material, the funding of surveys to assess the progress of the election campaign and to locate support, and in general organisation, limits the electorate's freedom of choice.

The final meaning of "representative" is concerned with the attitudinal and socio-economic characteristics of an organisation or body of persons compared with the characteristics of the larger organisations or body of persons they purport to represent. In the case of Parliament it is a matter of seeing how far MPs reflect the characteristics of the electorate. This usually means comparing the ages, occupations, education and other characteristics with those of the electorate, but it can also involve a comparison of the respective attitudes of MPs and the electorate by trying to answer the question: to what extent do MPs reflect public opinion? This may be distinguished from the first meaning of the term "representative", where the representative is expected to advocate the views of those he represents, in that the third meaning is concerned with how far he holds the same views as those he represents.

In what sense then is the Member of Parliament a representative? The classic statement is found in Edmund Burke's *Speech to the Electors of Bristol* in 1774:

> It ought to be the happiness and glory of a representative to live in the strictest union, the closest correspondence, and the most unreserved communication with his constituents. Their wishes ought to have great weight with him, their opinion high respect, their business unremitted attention. It is his duty to sacrifice his repose, his pleasures, his satisfaction to theirs; and above all, in all cases to prefer their interest to his own. But his unbiased opinion, his mature judgement, his enlightened conscience, he ought not to sacrifice to you, to any man, or to any set of men living. . . . Your representative owes you not his industry only, but his judgement, and he betrays instead of serving you, if he sacrifices it to your opinion.[2]

Burke's view of the role of the member was inevitably paralleled by his view of Parliament:

> Parliament is not a congress of ambassadors from different and hostile interests, which interests each must maintain as an agent and advocate against other agents and advocates; but Parliament is a deliberative assembly of one nation, with one interest, that of

the whole, where not local purposes, not local prejudices, ought
to guide, but the general good resulting from the general reason of
the whole. You choose a member indeed; but when you have
chosen him he is not the member for Bristol, but he is a member of
Parliament.[3]

The idea that Parliament should be a microcosm of the nation was
rejected by Burke, but Burke did acknowledge that it was his task to
defend and advance the interests of his electors, in spite of the fact
that he refused to accept instructions from them. By so doing, he also
claimed that it was his task to define those interests and how they
might best be defended and advanced. Whenever an MP is faced
with demands that he should support a policy of which he dis-
approves, or is threatened with dismissal by his local party, he is likely
to summon the ghost of Edmund Burke to his defence.

Burke's conception of the MP was and is a counsel of perfection.
Ironically it was Burke who defined a party as "a body of men
united for promoting by their joint endeavour the national interest,
upon some particular principle upon which they are all agreed"[4],
which is probably the best theoretical justification for party discipline. Yet it is largely because of the existence of parties that Burke's
advice is impractical. Burke followed his own advice and was a poor
party man; and parties now demand what eighteenth-century electors
once demanded of their MPs.

The overwhelming majority of MPs owe their election to the fact
that they stood as candidates pledged to support a particular party,
and that the overwhelming majority of voters choose between parties
rather than candidates. Only a handful of independent candidates
have been elected to Parliament since 1945 and most of these were
elected in 1945 and did not survive the 1950 general election. It can,
of course, be argued that the poor electoral record of independent
candidates has increasingly discouraged such candidates from
standing, but independents have quite frequently stood at by-
elections though voters have shown little inclination to support them.
This is in spite of the fact that by-elections do not normally determine the fate of governments in the House of Commons and voters
may "safely" desert their normal party allegiances. In most cases
such desertions accrue to a third party, such as the Liberal-SDP
Alliance or the Scottish or Welsh Nationalists. The few independent

candidates elected at general elections since 1950 have all been party rebels of one sort or another. Sir David Robertson was elected as an independent Conservative at Caithness and Sutherland in 1959, but was unopposed by the Conservative Party; S.O. Davies was elected as independent Labour member for Merthyr Tydvil in 1970, after the local Labour Party had refused to readopt him as official Labour candidate on grounds of age; and Edward Milne was elected as independent Labour member for Blyth in February 1974, when he too was refused readoption following a bitter personal dispute within the local Labour Party.

The most celebrated case in recent years is that of Dick Taverne, who was refused readoption by the Lincoln Labour Party mainly because of his support for British entry into the Common Market, although the dispute was also marked by bitter personal antagonism between Taverne and some of the local party officials. In October 1972 Taverne resigned his seat in order to bring about a by-election, which he won by a substantial majority in March 1973 against Labour, Conservative and Liberal opposition. In the general election of February 1974 Taverne retained Lincoln with a much reduced majority, but was defeated by the Labour candidate in October 1974. Taverne differed from the other "independents" in that for the most part they continued to support their erstwhile parties in the House of Commons, though they did not receive the party whip. Taverne's break with his party was complete, and he subsequently sought to establish a new party, the Campaign for Social Democracy, which put up several candidates in February 1974.

The Taverne case raised once again the argument whether an MP should regard himself and be regarded by his constituents as a representative or a delegate. There were, however, two separate questions. First, should the Lincoln Labour Party have the right to insist that Dick Taverne should support policies with which he did not personally agree? Second, should the Lincoln Labour Party have the right to dismiss Taverne as its candidate? Logically if the answer to the first question is "Yes", then the answer to the second must be "Yes", but the reverse is not true. If the Burkean doctrine prevails and the Lincoln Labour Party is denied the right of issuing instructions to Taverne, this does not preclude the party from dismissing him if it does not approve of his conduct as a member of Parliament.

The problem can perhaps be seen more clearly if we consider the case of MPs who "cross the floor" of the House of Commons and join another party. In 1962, for example, Alan Brown, who had been elected Labour member for Tottenham in 1959, resigned the Labour whip and joined the Conservative Party. He continued as a Conservative MP until 1964, when he was defeated at Tottenham. Similarly, in 1974 Christopher Mayhew, who, apart from a short break in 1950, had been a Labour MP since 1945, left the Labour Party to join the Liberals. In both these cases the local constituency Labour Parties took the view that the MP should resign and, if he chose, present himself to the electorate at a by-election, which is precisely what Dick Taverne did, though not at the behest of his local party. Brown refused to do so and effectively adopted a Burkean position as a representative; Christopher Mayhew stated that normally he would have resigned, but that he anticipated a general election in the autumn of 1974 and that his resignation would leave his constituents unrepresented since it was extremely unlikely that the Labour Party (whose decision it would be) would hold a by-election with the general election so near. Then in 1976 two Labour MPs, James Sillars and John Robertson, resigned the Labour whip to form the separate Scottish Labour Party. Neither resigned to fight a by-election under their new label and Sillars was defeated and Robertson did not stand in the general election of 1979. A more celebrated case, however, was that of Reg Prentice, Labour MP for Newham North-East and a former Cabinet minister, who was rejected by his constituency Labour Party, following a bitter and much-publicised struggle involving criticism of Prentice's support for the Common Market and other "right-wing" or "moderate" policies and counter-accusations of infiltration of the local Labour Party by left-wing extremists. His ultimate response was to "cross the floor" in October 1977 and join the Conservatives. Unlike most "floor-crossers", however, Prentice did not suffer defeat at the next election, but sought and won a safe Conservative seat in the 1979 election and subsequently served as a Minister of State in Mrs Thatcher's Government.

These cases, however, pale beside the defection or "floor-crossings" that followed the formation of the Social Democratic Party in 1981. Two of the original "Gang of Four" who set up the Council for Social Democracy in January 1981 – David Owen and William Rodgers – were Labour MPs. The other two, Shirley Williams and Roy Jenkins, both former Labour MPs, were subsequently elected in by-elections at

Crosby in 1981 and Glasgow (Hillhead) in 1982 respectively. A further twenty-six MPs "crossed the floor" and joined the SDP, of whom twenty-five were Labour and only one, Christopher Brocklebank-Fowler, a Conservative. Of the twenty-eight MPs who "crossed the floor" to join the SDP only one, Bruce Douglas-Mann, resigned to fight a by-election under the new label and was defeated for his pains. Thus in recent years MPs who have "crossed the floor" have invariably refused to resign and fight by-elections, despite frequent calls to do so. Only four of the remaining twenty-seven sitting MPs who joined the SDP were re-elected in 1983; one retired, whilst Roy Jenkins successfully defended his seat, but Shirley Williams was defeated at Crosby. Most of those MPs who "crossed the floor" to join the SDP defended their decisions to remain in Parliament by arguing that they had remained faithful to the manifesto on which they had fought the last election and that it was their former party which had shifted its ground. Their opponents dismissed this view, replying that they had been elected as candidates of a particular party, which they, the defectors, had now deserted.

The dilemma created by the MP who is elected under a party label which he subsequently rejects illustrates the dual role that the member of Parliament plays as a representative, one individual and the other collective. In the first role the MP is the representative of a territorial constituency and a defined number of constituents whose interests he seeks to defend and advance; in the second the MP is both a national representative and a party representative seeking to defend and advance the national interest and the interests of his party. In theory, and for the most part in practice, he defends and advances those interests as he perceives them and not as he may be instructed: the MP is a representative not a delegate.

The Burkean view of the MP cannot ultimately be sustained in the face of party and its need to survive. Just as we can ask whether the party should have the right to dismiss an MP, so we can also ask whether the MP has the right to refuse to accept party policy and still claim its support and protection. Clearly reality must lie somewhere between these two positions and there must be provision for dialogue, discussion and disagreement over policy within the party. For the MP to be threatened with dismissal every time he disagrees or criticises party policy would be intolerable, but it is equally intolerable for the party to continue to succour a member of Parliament who totally or substantially rejects its policies, and it is a matter of judgment when that point has been reached.

How representative is Parliament?

It is well known that Parliament is not a microcosm of the nation, and in this sense is an unrepresentative body. Clearly the House of Lords, consisting as it does of hereditary peers, life peers, Law Lords and bishops, cannot be representative of the nation. Indeed, it is doubtful if the nearly four hundred peers who attend one sitting of the House in three, are representative of the more than a thousand peers eligible to attend. Of these regular attenders about two-fifths are Conservatives, a quarter are Labour peers, about 12 per cent are Liberal-SDP supporters and the rest, a fifth, sit on the crossbenches and take no party whip. The Conservatives therefore do not have an overall majority, although their numbers are sometimes reinforced by less frequent attenders. More to the point is that Labour is in a position of permanent minority and the crossbenchers often play a crucial role in determining the outcome of deliberations by the Lords. It is therefore misleading to assume that the House of Lords is a constant and frequent source of Conservative obstruction to a Labour government with a majority in the House of Commons. With an assured majority in the Commons any government can ultimately overcome the opposition of the Lords by invoking the Parliament Acts of 1911 and 1949, although the upper house usually defers to the Commons if the latter reaffirms its view on any legislation. Nonetheless, the Labour Government of 1974–79 was more vulnerable, since it lacked a majority in the House of Commons for much of its period of office. Moreover, on a number of issues, such as trade union policy and devolution, Labour could not rely on the support of all its MPs and the Conservative opposition in both houses was not averse to taking advantage of this and of the lack of a Labour majority in the House of Lords. A growing antipathy towards the upper house led the Labour Party Conference to adopt a policy of abolishing the House of Lords and, although abolition was excluded from the party's election manifesto in 1979, an unequivocal commitment was made in the 1983 manifesto. It should not be thought, however, that Conservative governments are immune from changes made by the House of Lords: Mrs Thatcher and her colleagues were defeated on no less than forty-five occasions between 1979 and 1983.

Table 4.1   The socio-economic structure of the House of Commons elected in 1983

	Cons. %	Lab.%	Lib.	SDP	Other*	Total %
A. Age						
Under 30	1.5(6)	—	1	1	—	1.2(8)
30–39	19.4(77)	11.9(25)	6	—	6	17.5(114)
40–49	35.0(139)	30.6(64)	4	3	7	33.4(217)
50–59	31.5(125)	35.9(75)	5	1	5	32.5(211)
60–69	11.6(46)	18.7(39)	1	1	2	13.7(89)
70 or over	1.0(4)	2.9(6)	—	—	1	1.7(11)
Total	100.0(397)	100.0(209)	17	6	21	100.0(650)
B. Education						
University						
graduates	73.3(291)	50.7(106)	11	4	7	64.5(419)
Oxbridge						
graduates	46.3(184)	13.9(29)	4	3	1	34.0(221)
Attended public						
school	70.0(278)	14.4(30)	10	2	3	49.7(323)
C. Occupation						
Professions	34.2(136)	37.3(78)	11	2	10	36.3(237)
Business	51.1(203)	6.2(13)	3	—	9	35.2(228)
Miscellaneous	13.9(55)	21.5(45)	3	4	—	16.5(107)
Workers	0.8(3)	34.9(73)	—	—	2	12.0(78)
Total	100.0(397)	99.9(209)	17	6	21	100.0(650)

* Others consist of Official Unionist Party (11), Democratic Unionist Party (3), Scottish Nationalist (2), Welsh Nationalist (2), Social Democratic and Labour Party (1), Ulster Popular Unionist Party (1), and Sinn Fein (1).

In many cases it was on relatively minor issues, but there were also important defeats on trade union legislation. In 1983–84 the government suffered a further twenty reverses at the hands of the Lords, including legislation to cancel elections to the Greater London Council and the metropolitan county councils as a prelude to their abolition.

As an elected body with a fairly regular and substantial turnover, the House of Commons might be expected to be more representative of the nation than the House of Lords, but, as Table 4.1 suggests, it is far from being a microcosm of the nation.

The most unrepresentative feature of the House of Commons is the small number of women MPs of whom in 1983 there were twenty-three (3.5 per cent), notwithstanding the election of Britain's first woman Prime Minister in 1979. Indeed, the largest number and proportion ever elected was in 1964, when there were twenty-nine (4.6 per cent) women members. The explanation appears to lie in both supply and demand. There are probably fewer women than men who wish and actively seek to become parliamentary candidates, and there is undoubtedly a significant degree of prejudice against women candidates on the part of local parties, who often feel that being a candidate, and more particularly an MP, is a man's job. The two also affect each other and women are probably discouraged from seeking selection and the efforts of an all-party pressure group, the '300 Group', to secure the election of substantially more women have yet to bear fruit.

That the House of Commons does not mirror the electorate in terms of age is hardly surprising; only two age groups in the adult population, those between thirty and thirty-nine and between sixty and sixty-nine, were represented in the same proportions among MPs in 1983; those under thirty or seventy or over were considerably underrepresented, especially the younger group which comprises 20 per cent of the population and only 1 per cent of MPs. This meant that two-thirds of the MPs elected in 1983 were between forty and fifty-nine, twice the proportion of those age groups in the adult population. This is largely the result, on the one hand, of the need for almost all would-be MPs to gain experience of life, work and politics before local parties are willing to adopt them as candidates, especially for seats they can be expected to win; and on the other hand, of the fact that among existing MPs few wish to stand for re-election over the age of seventy and in some cases are discouraged from doing so by their local parties.

Despite the different age distributions between MPs and the adult population, on the whole sharper differences emerge when educational and occupational backgrounds are compared. Moreover, there are significant differences between the parties. More than three-fifths of the MPs elected in 1983 were university graduates, and over a third were graduates of either Oxford or Cambridge. Of the adult population only 5 per cent are university graduates. Similarly, if we express the number of Oxbridge graduates among MPs as a percentage of all graduate MPs and compare it with the number of undergraduates at Oxford and Cambridge in 1983 as a percentage of all undergraduates, the figures are respectively 52.7

per cent for MPs and 7.5 per cent for undergraduates. Even if allowance were made for the fact the rapid expansion of universities since
the early 1960s has meant that Oxford and Cambridge have a smaller
share of the undergraduate population, it would make little impact
on this statistic.

A similar pattern emerges if we note that nearly half the MPs
attended public schools, compared with approximately 5 per cent of
the adult population, but it should be noted that the great majority of
these MPs were Conservatives, although the proportion of Labour
MPs who attended public schools is nearly three times the national
average. The contrast between the two major parties is also seen in
that nearly three-quarters of the Conservatives compared with half the
Labour members were university graduates, and that nearly half the
Conservatives but only a seventh of the Labour MPs were Oxbridge
graduates.

It is equally clear that a House of Commons in which only one
MP in eight is a worker by occupation, and in which more than
two-thirds are either members of the professions or businessmen,
cannot be representative of the working population. Once again there
is a contrast between the two major parties, with all but three of the
workers being Labour MPs, all but thirteen of the businessmen being
Conservatives, and with more members of the professions and those
with miscellaneous occupations among Labour members.

The House of Commons is in strict socio-economic terms a
socially unrepresentative body, and this can be vividly illustrated by
analysing MPs according to the Hall-Jones scale of occupational
prestige which ranks occupations in seven classes, one of which is
subdivided into two. Approximately four-fifths of the population
are found in Classes 4–7, but over two-thirds of the MPs elected in
1983, including nearly 90 per cent of the Conservatives and nearly 50 per
cent of Labour MPs, are in Classes 1 and 2. While Labour MPs are a
more representative cross-section than Conservatives, they hardly
constitute a representative cross-section of the nation. It is almost
certainly true that if Labour MPs were placed in social classes
according to their parental background many more would be
classified as working-class, but this would neither entirely eliminate
the unrepresentativeness of Labour MPs, nor would it remove the
facts of their educational and occupational background, although it
would mark them off even more sharply from Conservative MPs. It
is also doubtful whether most of their constituents would regard

middle-class Labour MPs with working-class parents as other than middle-class. The House of Commons is thus a substantially middle-class body and has become increasingly so in the postwar period as the number of clearly working-class Labour MPs has declined.

The extent to which MPs represent public opinion on particular issues is discussed in Chapter 6, but it is worth discussing in the context of MPs being a microcosm of the nation the extent to which they represent groups in society and the broad spectrum of public opinion. Some members formally represent particular pressure or interest groups in Parliament, the best-known group being the trade union sponsored MPs in the Labour Party. In some cases a group will pay a member an annual fee or retainer to represent its interests in Parliament: this practice is followed, for instance, by the Police Federation and the National Association of Bookmakers. Such a relationship is not normally venal: the MP is often interested in the policy area concerned, his connection is usually well known, at least among his fellow members, and it is a convention in the House that Members declare any pecuniary interest in matters on which they speak. Other groups rely on the unpaid assistance of friendly and sympathetic MPs, and this is common among groups who exist to promote particular causes, and also with groups whose finances are limited; the National Council for Civil Liberties fulfils both these criteria, for example. In many instances such relationships cut across party lines – the Police Federation has had successive parliamentary spokesmen from the two major parties in the 1960s and early 1970s: James Callaghan (Labour 1955–64), Eldon Griffiths (Conservative 1966–70 and since 1974) and Alfred Morris (Labour 1971–74). Most major pressure groups have formally or informally recognised parliamentary spokesmen, and those which do not, or which like the Abortion Law Reform Society and the Society for the Protection of the Unborn Child, are created in response to legislative or other policy proposals, rapidly acquire spokesmen when the need arises. All members, of course, have a variety of interests, and those who are not recognised parliamentary spokesmen are often members of or have contact with the appropriate pressure groups.

There is no doubt that pressure groups are widely represented in Parliament, in both Lords and Commons, but how far they are represented in proportion to their numbers (where they have members) or their importance is another matter and very difficult to assess. In the first place Parliament's influence over policy is limited and the major, and most powerful groups work first and foremost through Whitehall (with whom they have long-standing arrangements for mutual consultation) and the government of the day (in whose hands the power of decision basically lies). Parliamentary representatives are therefore partly a useful adjunct to these contacts and their use may indicate a failure to secure their ends through the normal channels; or the matter may be the subject of a private bill or a private member's bill. In the second place the representation of a group is not necessarily more effective because it has a large membership and is wealthy, and less effective because it has few members and is poor. Much depends on other factors, such as organisational efficiency, the use of the appropriate techniques and procedures, and a knowledge of how Parliament works. Finally, there is the problem of cause and effect: the fact that roughly two-thirds of Conservative MPs have business interests in the form of company directorships, or that almost two-fifths of Labour MPs are union-sponsored, does not constitute proof that a particular decision was taken because of this; the relationships between the Conservative Party and business and the Labour Party and the trade unions are infinitely more complex than these facts of representation.

The extent to which Parliament represents the broad spectrum of public opinion is even more difficult to judge. That within the two major parties the broad strands of *party* opinion in terms of right and left are represented is undeniable: in the Conservative Party there is the Monday Club and the Tory Reform Group and in the Labour Party the Manifesto Group and the Tribune Group, whilst in the past there have been the Conservatives' One Nation Group and Labour's Campaign for Democratic Socialism, the Keep Left Group and Victory for Socialism. Outside the right–left spectrum nationalism has more recently found a voice in Parliament with the election of Welsh and Scottish Nationalists and MPs supported by the various Northern Ireland parties. It is, however, a pertinent question (and as yet one to which no satisfactory answer has been produced) to ask whether there is a "silent majority" unrepresented or significantly under- represented in Parliament.

How do MPs get there?
The short answer is, of course, that MPs are elected, but, apart from the viscissitudes of elections, before they are elected they are selected.

There are two crucial facts about the selection of parliamentary candidates: first, selection is primarily the concern of the local constituency party rather than the national party headquarters; and second, at least two-thirds of the seats in the House of Commons are either safe Conservative or safe Labour constituencies.

The basic role of the national party headquarters in selection is to lay down the ground rules and to retain a veto on the final selection. In both major parties the ground rules are concerned mainly with such matters as who may apply for a vacancy (in the case of the Conservatives) or who may nominate an individual as a possible candidate (in the case of Labour); what procedures should be followed; and who may participate in selecting the candidate. Although there are differences between the parties, both use a mixture of selection and election: a small or fairly small body sifts through the applicants or nominees and recommends a short-list for consideration by a larger body, which consists of representatives (called but not necessarily acting as delegates in the Labour Party) of the various bodies which constitute a local party (wards, trade union groups, youth and women's organisations etc.). This body (the Conservative Executive Council and the Labour Party General Management Committee) then hears each potential candidate give a short speech and answer questions, after which it elects one candidate by exhaustive ballot. The Liberals use a similar process, but the SDP has widened the selection process to allow all local party members to participate by means of a series of general meetings and postal ballots. The practice of allowing a general meeting of the local party members to make the final choice from a short-list has been used by an increasing number of local Conservative associations in recent years, though it remains the practice of only a minority – about a quarter of those selecting candidates for the 1983 election.

The national party headquarters maintain lists of "suitable" candidates (persons who have expressed the wish to become party candidates), but these lists do not serve as a means of foisting candidates on unwilling local parties. They provide the national party with a means of maintaining a qualitative check on candidates and of supplying local parties with names for consideration. Sinister as this might sound, the quality threshold is relatively low and the number of names suggested or contained on the list quite large. The lists are not particularly useful devices for securing the selection of candidates favoured by the party headquarters. Furthermore, any suggestion that the latter favours a candidate is likely to be counterproductive. During selection headquarters keeps a watching brief to ensure that the party rules are adhered to and the final choice is subject to endorsement by the national party. In practice the latter only rarely exerts its veto, as the Conservatives did with two Powellite candidates in February 1974 and another in October 1974, or as Labour did with an extreme left-wing candidate shortly before the election of 1966. Ironically, in those few cases where it is used the veto is often applied to candidates in seats which the party has little or no chance of winning, but the national party remains nonetheless conscious of its image.

The threat of an MP once-elected being rejected by his party is, in fact, much greater at local than at national level. This is true in both major parties, but Labour MPs tend to be more vulnerable than Conservatives, mainly because of sharper ideological differences in the Labour Party. Thus seven Labour MPs were refused readoption by their constituency parties between 1970 and 1979, mostly because of disagreements over policy, compared with one Conservative who retired under pressure from his local association. The pressure on Labour MPs increased after the 1979 election with the adoption of mandatory reselection for all sitting members once during the lifetime of each Parliament. As a result eight Labour MPs were refused readoption by their local parties for the 1983 election.

Local autonomy in selection is jealously guarded, especially by the incumbent party in safe seats since selection is tantamount to election, because in the country at large and in each constituency a majority of electors support *parties* rather than individual candidates. In safe seats the electorate's choice is pre-empted by the incumbent party's selection of a candidate and in marginal seats the electorate's choice is invariably limited to the candidates selected by the two major parties. The more volatile voting behaviour of the electorate, which began in the mid-1950s, gathered speed in the 1960s and continued into the 1970s and 1980s, has changed this to some extent. For the most part, however, it has not resulted in increased three-party or multi-party competition at *local* level. In a significant number of constituencies local two-party competition between Conservatives and Labour has been replaced by local two-party competition in which one of the two major parties (the one unsuccessfully challenging the incumbent party) is pushed into third place by the Liberal-SDP Alliance, or the Welsh or Scottish Nationalists, who then become the main challengers in that constituency. This has led to a further development in which Conservative or Labour supporters who find their party in third place are encouraged to desert it at the next election for the new challenger in order to maximise the vote *against* the Labour or Conservative "enemy". This phenomenon is known as "tactical voting". The effective intervention of third parties has resulted in the election of more third-party candidates. In February 1974 third-party intervention prevented either major party gaining a majority and in October 1974 limited Labour to a majority of only three, which was later eradicated through by-election losses. The result was two periods of minority government – from February to October 1974 and from 1976 to 1979, a situation which a number of observers saw as a good thing. However, it has not changed the basic facts that the electorate's choice is limited by the process of candidate selection and the working of the electoral system which guarantees the election of a large proportion of candidates.

The British electoral system is a simple and crude instrument usually known as the "first past the post" system, or the simple plurality. In any constituency the candidate with the most votes wins, but because a candidate wins whether he has a majority of one or many thousands it is usual for the relationship between the *national* vote and the distribution of seats among the parties to become distorted. Thus a party may win some constituencies by very substantial majorities, but if its opponent can win sufficient seats by very *small* majorities it can secure a majority of the seats in the House of Commons and yet have less than half the national vote. This is much more likely to happen if third parties compete in elections, and the larger their share of the vote the more likelihood there is of distortion between seats and votes. Furthermore, unless the support for a third party is heavily concentrated in a limited number of constituencies (which enables it to maximise its impact) or unless it secures about 30 per cent of the national vote, the proportion of seats it wins is always substantially less than its share of the national vote. In short, as Table 4.2 illustrates, Britain does not have a system of proportional representation.

We can see from Table 4.2 that no party secured an absolute

Table 4.2   The distribution of votes and seats at general elections between 1945 and 1983

Election	Cons. Votes %	Cons. Seats %	Labour Votes %	Labour Seats %	Liberal Votes %	Liberal Seats %	Other Votes %	Other Seats %	No. of seats
1945	39.6	32.8	48.0	61.4M	9.0	1.9	3.4	3.9	640
1950	43.5	47.7	46.1	50.4M	9.1	1.4	1.3	0.5	625
1951	48.0	51.3M	48.8	47.2	2.6	1.0	0.6	0.5	625
1955	49.7	54.8M	46.4	44.0	2.7	0.9	1.2	0.3	630
1959	49.3	57.9M	43.9	41.0	5.9	0.9	0.9	0.2	630
1964	43.4	48.3	44.1	50.3M	11.2	1.4	1.3	—	630
1966	41.9	40.1	48.1	57.8M	8.5	1.9	1.5	0.2	630
1970	46.4	52.3M	43.1	45.7	7.5	1.0	3.0	1.0	630
1974 (Feb)	38.1	46.6	37.2	47.4m	19.3	2.2	5.4	3.8	635
1974 (Oct)	35.7	43.5	39.3	50.2M	18.3	2.0	6.7	4.2	635
1979	43.9	53.4M	36.9	42.4	13.8	1.7	5.4	2.5	635
1983	42.4	61.1M	27.6	32.2	25.4*	3.5*	4.6	3.2	650

M – majority government;   m – minority government.
* Liberal-SDP Alliance

majority of the national vote at any general election between 1945 and 1983, but with the exception of February 1974, one party always secured a majority of the seats in the House of Commons. Thus in spite of its massive majority of 137 seats in 1945 the Labour Party did not win a majority of the national vote, whilst the Conservatives in 1983 won an even larger majority, 144, with little more than two-fifths of the votes cast. Only four times this century has one party or electoral coalition won a majority of seats *and* votes: in 1900, 1918, 1931 and 1935. In two cases since 1945, 1951 and February 1974, the party which secured most seats was not the party with the most votes, though a crude form of justice operated in that in one case the Conservatives and in the other Labour benefited. In proportionate terms, however, third parties have always suffered the greatest injustices. In February 1974 the Welsh Nationalists and to a much greater extent the Scottish Nationalists benefited from the relative concentration of their support, but the Liberals, whose support is more widespread, secured no less than 19.3 per cent of the vote and were rewarded with a mere 2.2 per cent of the seats. The crudity of the electoral system is well illustrated by the fate of the Liberals since 1964: in 1964 they won 11.2 per cent of the vote and nine seats; in 1966 their vote fell to 8.5 per cent but the number of seats rose to twelve; in 1970 their vote fell by 1 per cent to 7.5 per cent, but the number of seats fell to six; in February 1974 they nearly trebled their vote to 19.3 but little more than doubled their seats to fourteen; and in October 1974 their vote dropped slightly to 18.3 per cent and they suffered a net loss of three seats. In terms of electoral proportionality an even greater injustice occurred in the 1983 election in that Labour won 209 seats with 27.6 per cent of the vote and the Liberal-SDP Alliance won a mere 23 seats with 25.4 per cent of the vote.

It has been calculated that had the single transferable vote – the most likely form of proportional representation to be adopted in Britain – been in operation, a party with 48 per cent or more of the votes cast would have secured an absolute majority of seats in the House of Commons. Given the figures shown in Table 4.2 and assuming the electorate would have voted in the same proportions, then in five out of the twelve elections held since 1945 one party would have had an absolute majority of seats. In terms of completed Parliaments between 1945 and 1983 there would have been single-party majority government for about three-fifths of the time but *none* since 1970. It can, of course, be argued that if proportional representation had been in operation then the electorate might have voted differently, but it hardly seems likely that proportional representation would have encouraged the electorate to neglect third parties even more than they did under the simple plurality. Naturally it is not in the interests of either of the two major parties to introduce proportional representation unless one of them wishes to try to form an anti-Conservative or anti-Labour coalition, as the case may be.

The two major parties defend the electoral system principally on the grounds that the electorate prefers "strong government", which is equated with *majority* government and with *party* government in the sense that the government is formed by one party. They acknowledge that minority government is one-party government, but it, of course, has the weakness of lacking a majority in its own right; and they object to coalition government on the grounds that it is not government by one party, the divisions between the parties become blurred, and the resulting policies are unsatisfactory. A majority government may be a "strong" government in that it can normally secure the passage of its programme through Parliament, but it does not necessarily make it a "strong" government in terms of being an *effective* government. The desire of any party, not least the Conservative and Labour Parties, to secure a majority and to govern unfettered by coalition or a minority situation is perfectly understandable, but if the electorate were to persist in denying any party a majority it becomes an unattainable desire. Moreover, the more frequently the electorate does this and therefore deprives the electoral system of its principal justification, the greater will be the pressure for reform of the electoral system.

Should proportional representation eventually be adopted it could have a profound affect on the operation of Parliament. Most obviously proponents of PR argue that the House of Commons would be a more representative body in terms of representing the electorate's party preferences, but what types of governments would emerge depends largely on those party preferences. Recent elections have shown a marked fall in the share of the vote won by the two major parties – the last occasion when one party secured more than 48 per cent of the votes cast was in 1966. Minority government would certainly become more likely, but *coalition* government might eventually become the norm. Coalition government, however, can take many forms: two or more parties might cooperate to form a stable majority government virtually as secure as any single-party government, as has been the norm in West Germany; conversely, instability would be likely where sufficient parties were unable to agree on common policies or where one or more of the parties were reluctant coalition partners, as in Belgium or the Netherlands; one of the major parties might find itself constantly or invariably in government or opposition, as is the case with the Christian Democrats and the Communists in Italy; and so on. It is by no means easy to predict what would happen in Britain, especially since the emergence of the Social Democratic Party and the formation of the Liberal-SDP Alliance. Within Parliament the traditional divide between government and opposition might have to be reviewed: already the Alliance in general and the Social Democrats in particular have been demanding recognition more in accordance with their electoral support rather than their representation in the House of Commons.

Does it matter whether Parliament is representative?

Parliament is not socio-economically representative of the electorate, but whether this is of any consequence is a matter of opinion. One view is that the test should not be representativeness, but whether or not the process of selection and election produces "good" MPs. By "good" is meant MPs who effectively carry out the role of Member of Parliament. As we have already seen, there is some dispute as to what that role is, but leaving this aside, it is not difficult to find among MPs agreement that X is a "good" constituency member, Y is a "good" debater, Z is a "good" committee man, and so on. Unfortunately, it is not at all clear what, if any, socio-economic characteristics contribute to making X, Y and Z "good" constituency members, debaters or committee men. There is some circumstantial evidence that particular MPs win or lose support on personal grounds, and this may well be related to such factors as whether or not they are effective constituency members, but for the most part the local electorate knows little or nothing of how its member performs in Parliament. There is a good deal of evidence that incumbent local parties are fully aware that they almost certainly are (in safe seats) or may be (in marginal seats) selecting a Member of Parliament, but there is rather less evidence that their choice is determined or much affected by the job that MPs are expected to carry out. Certainly some parties have been swayed by the desire to select someone who will look after the constituency, or have been impressed by a potential candidate's speaking ability, or have detected ministerial material in a candidate, but it is very difficult, if not impossible, to gather systematic evidence.

Those who argue that the House of Commons should be a microcosm of the nation do so partly out of a belief that it is ultimately the only fair form of representation, and partly out of a belief that the House of Commons would be a better place for it. To secure microcosmic representation by electoral means is difficult since it involves giving the electorate the right to choose its representatives, but limiting that choice in order to ensure that a microcosm is elected. If the less exacting demand for proportional representation is considered, then it can only be resisted on the sort of pragmatic grounds mentioned earlier. The argument that the House of Commons would be improved by microcosmic representation is a different matter. Few would disagree that if the Commons were totally dominated by any particular social, ethnic, economic, ideological or other group it would be to the detriment of Parliament and the nation, but it is not dominated by any such group. Similarly, if a group of acknowledged importance in society had no means of making its views known in Parliament and clearly suffered, as a result, then few would support the continuance of such a situation, but this is not generally the case. It is, however, an assumption that a House of Commons that is socio-economically unrepresentative must carry out its functions less well than a House of Commons which is a microcosm of the nation. The House of Commons is not the legislative equivalent of an opinion poll: if it were, it would be cheaper and more efficient to abolish Parliament and transfer its functions to the Office of Population Censuses and Surveys.

What is much more to the point is that representation, like justice, should be seen to be done. This does not necessarily require that all MPs must become delegates, nor does it require mathematical precision in the electoral system and microcosmic representation. It does, however, assume acceptance by the electorate in general, and by those groups in society which seek representation, that the system is fair, for the system remains representative only as long as it is believed to be so.

5 Parliament and policy

Ministerial responsibility and policy

Parliamentary government is distinguished from other forms of government by being defined as *responsible* government in that the executive is constitutionally responsible to the legislature. Ministers are *collectively* responsible for the policies and conduct of the government and *individually* responsible for the policies and administration of their departments. Before we consider what this means in practice some mention should be made of two other meanings of the term "responsible", and again we turn to A.H. Birch:

> In the first place, the term "responsible" is commonly used to describe a system of government in which the administration is responsive to public demands and movements of public opinion. . . .
>
> In the second place, the term is used in a quite different way, which invokes the concepts of duty and moral responsibility.[1]

There is no doubt that in Britain governments are expected to respond to public opinion and that they are expected not to pursue irresponsible policies. It is not always easy to reconcile these two expectations: public opinion may demand policies which would, in the judgment of the government, be irresponsible; and policies which the government regards as responsible may be extremely unpopular with the public. Where does the government's duty lie? There is no easy answer to such a question, but it probably lies between two alternatives. First, if the government feels that it cannot implement a particular policy without widespread public support than it should resign or put its policy to the test of a general election. Second, if the government feels strongly about a particular policy and believes that it can be implemented despite its unpopularity, then it should go ahead with the policy and risk subsequently being turned out of office when an election is eventually held. Always to demand the resignation of the government in the face of widespread unpopularity would seem to demand that governments should abdicate the second meaning of "responsibility".

Ministerial responsibility is a product of convention and is the constitutional source of parliamentary scrutiny and control of the executive. Its relevance in this respect is clear if we consider Parliament's ability to scrutinise the nationalised industries. The government and the departmental ministers concerned accept overall responsibility for the nationalised industries, but they do not accept responsibility for their day to day administration on the grounds that such responsibility is not laid on them by the legislation which set up the nationalised industries. There is little doubt that if ministers could similarly repudiate responsibility in other spheres Parliament's ability to scrutinise and extract information from the government would be severely limited. As the basis of Parliament's scrutinising and informing function ministerial responsibility is therefore far from being a constitutional fiction; it is in fact a means to political reality.

There is also another sense in which it can be argued that ministerial responsibility is a constitutional fiction, or largely so, and that is the argument that ministerial responsibility will invariably be subordinated to the political solidarity of a government defending itself against its opponents. This can affect both collective and individual ministerial responsibility, but they are better dealt with separately.

The ultimate operation of collective responsibility can take one of three forms. First, where one or more ministers feel unable to accept a Cabinet decision they should resign; second, if a minister publicly criticises government policy the Prime Minister may demand his resignation; and third, if Parliament (in practice the House of Commons) considers that the government has adopted a bad policy or series of bad policies it may force the government to resign. The first and second forms do operate from time to time, the third only rarely.

In 1958, for instance, the Chancellor of the Exchequer (Peter Thorneycroft) and his two junior Treasury ministers (Enoch Powell and Nigel Birch) resigned because their views on economic policy were rejected by the Cabinet; Lord Longford left the Cabinet in 1968 when he felt unable to support the decision to postpone the school leaving age; Reg Prentice resigned as Minister for Overseas Development in 1969 because he wished to see an increase in overseas aid; in 1971 Edward Taylor resigned as Parliamentary Under-Secretary at the Scottish Office because he opposed British entry into the Common Market; Norman Buchan, Minister of State for Agriculture, resigned in 1974 over a government decision to transfer control over food prices from his department to the newly-created Department of Prices and Consumer Protection; in 1976 Joan Lestor, Under-Secretary at the Department of Education and Science, resigned in protest against education cuts; Albert Stallard, a government whip, resigned in 1979 because he opposed the government's proposal to increase the number of parliamentary constituencies in Northern Ireland; and, also involving a government whip and Northern Ireland, Nicholas Budgen resigned in 1982 because he was not prepared to support proposals for "rolling devolution" for the province. These are typical examples. They usually involve the minister directly responsible for the matter, but, as in the cases of Lord Longford, Edward Taylor, Albert Stallard and Nicholas Budgen ministers not directly concerned sometimes feel constrained to resign. In practice, however, ministers are under considerable pressure not to resign when they are unhappy about Cabinet decisions, since resignations are often evidence of a split in the government party, damaging to party morale, and a ready weapon in the hands of opponents. This pressure on the minister not to resign probably comes in good measure from within himself, as well as from ministerial colleagues and friends: he is, after all, a party man and, unless he has an ulterior motive, does not willingly risk splitting the party. Ministers do not therefore resign lightly and must usually feel very strongly before doing so.

It is sometimes said that for a minister to resign on grounds of collective responsibility is a form of political suicide and in some cases it is: the "offending" ex-minister never receives office again. It is certainly a form of premature retirement from office in some cases, such as that of Lord Longford, but the examples mentioned above also included Peter Thorneycroft, Enoch Powell, Reg Prentice and Edward Taylor, all of whom held office again, in three cases in the Cabinet. To resign over collective responsibility is honourable and an honourable resignation does not preclude rehabilitation.

Of course, not all ministers who disagree with government policy feel constrained to resign. On the contrary they feel impelled to make known their disagreement. This is sometimes done discreetly, or relatively so, by hints to friends on the backbenches, unattributable comments to the lobby correspondent of this newspaper or that, a speech to a party committee, and so on, and is regarded as part of the game of Cabinet politics. A minister or group of ministers may use such methods to secure support for what may be a minority view in the Cabinet, or to influence the Cabinet during a period when policy is being evolved, although the latter does not necessarily contravene collective responsibility. Discretion, however, is the watchword.

Early in 1967, for example, Douglas Jay, who was President of the Board of Trade and a known anti-Marketeer, was reported to have addressed the Parliamentary Labour Party's Finance and Economic Affairs Committee in terms which were critical of the Labour Government's decision to consider again the possibility of joining the Common Market. The Prime Minister, Harold Wilson, was in turn reported to have warned ministers that their comments must be in accordance with government policy towards the EEC or they must resign office. Later in 1967, when there was a government reshuffle, Douglas Jay was dropped from the government, a fate which may or may not have been connected with his earlier "indiscretion". Similarly, as a member of the 1974–79 Labour Cabinet, Tony Benn, first as Secretary of State for Industry and then for Energy, made skilful use of his position as Chairman of the Labour Party National Executive Committee's Home Policy Committee to express his disagreement with a number of government policies; and Mrs Thatcher's critics within her Cabinet, commonly known as the "wets", made their opposition to government economic policy widely known, though in due course most were quietly removed in ministerial reshuffles.

More rarely the Prime Minister may dismiss a minister who fails to observe collective responsibility. In 1975 Eric Heffer, Minister of State at the Department of Industry, was dismissed for speaking in the House of Commons against the Cabinet's decision to recommend that Britain should remain in the Common Market. Heffer, however, had already been "reminded" in 1974 of his constitutional position as a minister after he had publicly criticised the government's policy over the sale of frigates to Chile. More recently, in 1981, Keith Speed, Under-Secretary of Defence for the Navy, spoke publicly against naval cuts and was dismissed. There seems little doubt that in both cases the Prime Minister was determined to make an example of the offending minister.

These cases illustrate the impact of political solidarity on collective responsibility. Any minister who steps seriously and persistently out of line with government policy can be dismissed by the Prime Minister, but much depends on the circumstances. In fact Eric Heffer and Keith Speed are the only ministers this century who have been dismissed on the grounds that they have contravened the doctrine of collective responsibility. That a minister may escape instant dismissal is little consolation, for subsequently he may be more discreetly removed from office in a reshuffle and the mantle of martyrdom which instant dismissal may confer is obscured by the lapse of time and the more important news of the reshuffle. Yet more discreetly the minister may escape removal from office, but later find himself denied the hoped-for promotion, or the transfer to a department in which he has a close interest, or be faced with the unenviable choice of a lesser office or resignation. Instant dismissal may undermine political solidarity; it may be evidence of a split in the Cabinet or government which may lead to or be evidence of a split in the party. Considerations of political solidarity therefore usually prevail over the immediate operation of collective responsibility on the relatively few occasions that ministers contravene the doctrine.

The way in which collective responsibility phases into political solidarity is shown by the way in which the norms of collective responsibility tend to prevail in opposition, even though there is no *constitutional* obligation on opposition parties to observe them. Thus shadow ministers are expected to resign if they are unable to accept party policies and, more rarely, may be dismissed by the party leader if they publicly disagree with party policy. The most notable case in recent years was Edward Heath's dismissal in 1968 of Enoch Powell, following the latter's emphatic repudiation of the Conservative Party's immigration policy. But this was by no means an isolated instance: in 1979, whilst still Leader of the Opposition, Margaret Thatcher dismissed Winston Churchill from his post as an opposition spokesman for voting in favour of lifting economic sanctions against Rhodesia. Similarly, in 1982 Michael Foot dismissed three frontbench spokesmen, Tam Dalyell, Andrew Faulds and John Tilley, for defying the Shadow Cabinet's decision to abstain in a vote on the

Falklands crisis and in 1984 Neil Kinnock dismissed two opposition spokesmen, Frank Field and Martin Madden, for voting against government policy on trade union representation at GCHQ, rather than following the opposition line of abstaining.

Only rarely does the House of Commons enforce collective responsibility to the extent of forcing a government to resign. This last occurred in April 1979, when the minority Labour Government led by James Callaghan was defeated by a single vote, resulting in the calling of the general election of May 1979. Of course, for a minority government defeat in the House of Commons is an ever-present possibility, as the 1974–79 Labour Government found during most of its period of office. Ultimately, the government did fall as a result of an adverse vote in the Commons, but it survived a number of no-confidence motions in spite of suffering no fewer than seventy-four defeats in the division lobbies prior to its final downfall. The government survived because in most cases it accepted the policy changes consequent upon those defeats and, where appropriate, tabled confidence motions which it subsequently won. In addition, the government was sustained in office between March 1977 and July 1978 by the Lib-Lab Pact. The last occasion when a majority government was brought down through the operation of this convention was in 1940, when the then Prime Minister, Neville Chamberlain, resigned after widespread abstentions among his supporters. Even then the government won a majority in the division lobbies, but Chamberlain considered that his support had been so much reduced that he no longer had the confidence of his party and therefore of the House of Commons. Normally, if the government has a majority political solidarity ensures its survival.

Political solidarity operates in a similar way on individual ministerial responsibility. That ministers do accept responsibility for the policies and administration of their departments there is no doubt, at least in the sense that they speak for their departments in debates and answer questions in the House. Equally it is a bold minister (not to say a foolish one) who claims that all his policies are perfect and that no mistakes occur in his department. Ministerial resignations for reasons of individual responsibility are in practice somewhat infrequent. The most recent cases occurred in 1982, when four ministers resigned over two different issues. In January 1982 Nicholas

Fairbairn, the Solicitor-General for Scotland, resigned over the mishandling of a court case in which he made a statement to the press before making an announcement in Parliament. More importantly, in April 1982 the Foreign Secretary, Lord Carrington, the Lord Privy Seal, Humphrey Atkins, and the Minister of State at the Foreign Office with responsibility for Latin American affairs, Richard Luce, all resigned following the failure to anticipate the Argentine invasion of the Falklands. The last clearcut case before the Falklands resignations was that of Sir Thomas Dugdale, who, as Minister of Agriculture in 1954, accepted responsibility for errors in his department over the resale of land requisitioned during the Second World War. Altogether there have been only twenty-four such resignations since 1855. No resignations occurred over such matters as the fuel crisis of 1947, the failure of the groundnuts scheme in East Africa in 1949, the death of a number of Mau Mau prisoners at Hola Camp in 1958, or the excess profits made by Ferranti on the Bloodhound missile or the financial mismanagement by the Crown Agents under successive governments in the 1960s and 1970s. Of course, it can be argued that resignation should be reserved for the worst blunders, yet all those cited above were probably worse than Sir Thomas Dugdale's "errors" (those of a civil servant, in fact) or that of Nicholas Fairbairn, whose action was more of an embarrassment to the government than a serious policy failure. As for Lord Carrington and his two colleagues, they were subsequently able to claim exoneration following the publication of the Franks Report on the Falklands in 1983 and the minister most closely involved in relations with Argentina prior to the invasion, Richard Luce, was later restored to office. Each case is in a sense unique, but political solidarity often plays a part: invariably the government and its supporters rally to the defence of the minister under attack and protect him with their majority. In practice whether a minister resigns usually depends on three factors: how determined the minister himself is to resign or to resist resignation; whether the Prime Minister is prepared to accept or force the minister's resignation; and whether government supporters in the Commons are prepared to defend the minister.

As with collective responsibility other fates may await the "offending" minister and after a decent interval he may be quietly retired from office or moved to another post. Because an attack on one minister is usually construed as an attack on the government, political solidarity usually prevails and ministers who are found wanting are dealt with covertly rather than overtly.

Forcing the resignation of the government or bringing individual ministers to book are not in themselves important political weapons except in special circumstances: the political reality of ministerial responsibility lies not in its ultimate enforcement, but in making ministers render to Parliament an account of their responsibilities and how they have exercised them, and it is precisely because ministers are expected to defend their policies in Parliament that scrutiny of the executive is possible.

Parliament and legislation

As we have already seen, the government controls most of the time of the House of Commons and can usually ensure the passage of almost all its legislation. Most legislation therefore emanates from the government, but government bills are not simply a catalogue of the measures favoured by the party in power and even less do they originate mostly from the party's manifesto and election pledges. Apart from the annual bills which all governments must pass – the Finance and Appropriation Bills and the Consolidated Fund Bills – and those bills which consolidate or draw together into a single Act of Parliament a number of existing acts in a particular field, bills may originate from five major sources.

Obviously the governing party's manifesto and election pledges are a major source, but mainly in the early years of a Parliament. Thus in the 1967–68 session, eighteen months after the General Election of 1966, only one bill was introduced by the government in fulfilment of its manifesto, and in the following session none. Similarly, the first session of the 1979–83 Parliament was dominated by the Conservative election manifesto, with nearly a third of the government's bills arising from manifesto commitments, whereas this proportion dropped considerably in subsequent sessions.

Between elections all governments are faced with situations which they either did not or could not anticipate and which require legislative action, and these constitute a second source. In the summer of 1976, for instance, the Labour Government introduced a bill to deal with the problems arising from a prolonged drought and in 1980 the Conservative Government introduced the Iran (Temporary

Provisions) Bill to give it the power to prosecute those trading with Iran during the American hostages crisis. Governments may also decide to change policies, as both Conservative and Labour Governments did when they imposed incomes policies in 1972 and 1975–76 respectively.

Other problems become the subject of various types of inquiry, some temporary, others permanent. Royal commissions and committees of inquiry, for example, are a favourite device of governments when faced with complex problems on which they have no settled policy and no strong views, or they may be appointed to consider sensitive social, constitutional or other issues on which the government feels in need of guidance, or simply matters on which there is a dearth of information without which the government is reluctant to act. Added to this, of course, is the opportunity that such inquiries afford for the postponement of decisions with all the appearance of action whilst the inquiry proceeds: "Taking minutes," as Harold Wilson once said, "and lasting years." The Warnock Report of 1978 on the provision of education for handicapped children, which led directly to the Education Act, 1981 and the Stevens Committee, 1976, whose report on planning controls over mineral workings was implemented by the Town and Country Planning (Minerals) Act, 1981, are examples of such inquiries. There are also permanent bodies of inquiry, such as the Criminal Law Revision Committee, the Law Commission and the Royal Commission on Environmental Pollution, which produce legislative proposals from time to time, many of which become law.

Britain's membership of the Common Market also results in the need for legislative action. Apart from the European Communities Act, 1972, which, where appropriate, amended British legislation to conform with the Treaty of Rome, subsequent policy changes agreed by the member states of the EEC and consequent directives from the EEC Commission in Brussels often require the passing of legislation. Thus the Companies Act, the Film Act and the Insurance Companies Act passed in the 1979–80 session had their origins substantially or entirely in the EEC.

Finally, a great deal of legislation originates from government departments, some dealing with matters which civil servants working in particular fields bring to the attention of ministers, and some as a consequence of decisions made by ministers, policies already being pursued, or legislation already passed, all of which may necessitate further legislation. A decision affecting the funding of nationalised industries may require amending legislation for all the Acts establishing those industries, or international agreements may need legislative enforcement.

In practice some bills may originate from more than source. The setting up of an independent prosecution service by the Prosecution of Offences Act, 1985 had it origins in the Royal Commission on Criminal Procedure, which reported in 1981. The case for an independent prosecution service was accepted in the 1983 Conservative manifesto and legislation was foreshadowed in the 1984 Queen's Speech.

The legislative process can be divided into three stages: a preparatory stage, a parliamentary stage and a post-enactment stage. Although it would be misleading to suggest that Parliament is concerned only with the second of the three stages, its concern with the first and third stages is limited and variable. What is important to appreciate is that, although Parliament may properly be described as a legislature, it is only a *part* of the legislative process. Some observers would add that Parliament does not play the most important part in that process. In a sense this is true in that, with the limited exception of private members' (or peers') bills, Parliament does not initiate legislation and is not responsible for its implementation. Nonetheless, Parliament may play some part in the preparatory stage of legislation as one of the many sources of influence that may be brought to bear on proposed legislation and may also be involved in the post-enactment stage in reviewing where the legislative shoe pinches.

Legislation is normally the product of a complicated and long-drawn-out process, the stages of which are not difficult to describe in theory but are often difficult to unravel in practice. This is particularly true of the preparatory stage, largely because it takes place in private rather than public, but even in the basically public parliamentary stage it is not easy to answer the question, who did what, when, how and why? It may well be possible to discover who did what, when and how, but finding out exactly why is a formidable task. Ministers may stress that they have consulted various pressure groups, but they are often reluctant to admit that they have been influenced by any group in particular. Similarly, governments seldom acknowledge that their decisions are affected by backbench pressure in Parliament, yet they appear to listen assiduously enough. Conversely, pressure groups and backbenchers are quick to claim success whether it is in the appearance or the reality. There are so many factors involved in the making of a single decision by a minister – pressure groups, backbenchers, Cabinet colleagues, the party in the country, the government's priorities, the attitude of the opposition, the economic situation and so on almost *ad infinitum* – that to give each factor its proper weight and arrive at some "scientific" conclusion is probably impossible. Indeed it can be argued that each decision includes an element of uniqueness which defies generalisation, but this should not be allowed to prevent us from understanding how political decisions are reached.

The complex and long-drawn-out nature of the legislative process is illustrated in Table 5.1.

The influx of mainly coloured immigrants into Britain in the post-war period led in due course to the passing of the Immigration Act in 1962, but immigration control continued to be a significant policy concern of all governments, resulting in further legislation in 1968 to deal with the sudden influx of Kenyan Asians and a further general tightening of controls in 1971. Even so, immigration remained a major issue and during the 1970s the Conservative Party Annual Conference passed a number of motions urging yet more stringent controls. The issue was further complicated by the complex nature of British nationality law and this was recognised by the publication of a Green Paper or discussion document on the subject by the Labour Government in 1977. In its 1979 election manifesto Labour pledged itself to legislate on the Green Paper proposals, whilst the Conservatives promised new nationality legislation as a means of further controlling immigration.

At the preparatory stage the government may consult various pressure groups, but whether and at what point they are consulted varies. In some cases extensive consultation may occur during the drafting of a White Paper or a bill, but in other cases any interested parties must await the publication of the government's proposals or of the bill itself. In the case of the British Nationality Bill consultation with outside interests appears to have been limited, although the new Conservative Government did say that since the publication of the Green Paper in 1977 over four hundred comments and representa-

Table 5.1   The legislative process: the British Nationality Act, 1981

A.   The preparatory stage

1. 1973–79 – resolutions passed at a number of Conservative Party Annual Conferences urging greater limits on immigration.

2. April 1977 – Green Paper (i.e. discussion document), *British Nationality Law: Discussion of Possible Changes*, published by the Labour Government acknowledging that the law on nationality was in need of reform.

3. April 1979 – commitment to new nationality legislation included in the Conservative and Labour election manifestos.

4. 30 July 1980 – White Paper, *British Nationality Law: Outline of Proposed Legislation* published.

B.   The parliamentary stage

5. 20 November 1980 – commitment to introduce legislation included in the Queen's Speech.

6. 13 January 1981 – British Nationality Bill introduced in the House of Commons and given its first reading.

7. 28 January 1981 – second reading debate in the House of Commons.

8. 10 February 1981–14 May 1981 – committee stage of bill in standing committee meeting for 48 sittings.

9. 2–3 June 1981 – report stage of the bill in the House of Commons.

10. 4 June 1981 – third reading of the bill in the House of Commons.

11. 8 June–31 July 1981 – bill passes all its stages in the House of Lords.

12. 27 October 1981 – consideration of the Lords' amendments by the House of Commons.

13. 29 October 1981 – the House of Lords accepts the House of Commons' rejection of some Lords' amendments.

14. 30 October 1981 – British Nationality Bill receives the Royal Assent.

C.   The post-enactment stage

15. July 1982 – first statutory instruments under the British Nationality Act issued by the Home Secretary.

16. 1 January 1983 – British Nationality Act comes into force.

17. 28 March 1983 – British Nationality Act is amended by the British Nationality (Falklands Islands) Act, 1983.

---

tions had been received from members of the public and interested bodies. The publication of the White Paper in July 1980 was well-received in Conservative circles, but strongly criticised by the Labour opposition, by organisations representing Britain's coloured population and by a number of Commonwealth Governments.

The parliamentary stage took ten months (not unusual for a controversial bill) and resulted in several substantive changes to the original bill, though none altered its fundamental purpose. The most important change was probably that forced on the Government in the House of Lords by which citizens of Gibraltar were given the right to register as British citizens. This may not seem a very impressive result from the parliamentary scrutiny of an Act of Parliament of seventy-three pages, with fifty-three sections and nine schedules, which was the subject of a large number of amendments at its committee and report stages, with further amendments proposed in the Lords. It is, however, largely borne out by evidence submitted by government departments to the Select Committee on Procedure in 1970–71 in which it was estimated that of the forty-eight government bills passed in 1967–68 12 per cent were substantially amended, 39 per cent were slightly amended, another 39 per cent were negligibly amended, leaving 10 per cent with the substance of the bill left intact. An exhaustive study of legislation over three sessions of Parliament, *The Parliamentary Scrutiny of Legislation*[2] by Professor J.A.G. Griffith, provides conclusive evidence of the limited number of changes made to government bills by Parliament.

The post-enactment stage began with a series of statutory instruments setting up the machinery to implement the act, prior to its coming into force in January 1983, but perhaps the most interesting part of this stage was the passage in March 1983 of a further act amending the British Nationality Act to give Falkland Islanders British citizenship – a proposal which had narrowly failed on a tied vote in the House of Lords during the passage of the original bill in 1981. In the meantime, of course, the atmosphere had been totally changed by the Argentine invasion of the Falklands. What conclusions can be drawn from this and the fact that legislation is for the most part not substantially altered in its passage through Parliament?

Professor Griffith's research provides part of the answer: he found that in the 1967–68 and 1968–69 sessions 50 per cent of the bills were dealt with in between 8 and 9 per cent of the total time spent on legislation in the House of Commons. Conversely, this meant that 28 per cent of the bills in these sessions absorbed no less than between 75 and 81 per cent of the total time spent on legislation and there is no reason to believe that this situation has changed significantly since this research was completed. The principle reason is, of course, that controversial bills take longer, but in this context "controversial" means a bill which is strongly opposed by the official opposition. The theory that a bill is accepted in principle at the second reading and that subsequent stages are intended to examine how that principle can best be implemented, does not work out in practice if the opposition is determined to oppose the bill at every opportunity. The theory simply does not accord with the logic of party politics: if a party bitterly opposes the principle of a bill why should it assist in the more efficient implementation of that principle? There is also a more positive element: the stronger the feeling against the principle the more the opposing party will feel that the government should be forced to justify its proposals at every turn and in as much detail as possible. To argue that as a minority (however temporary) the opposition should accept the will of the majority merely raises the counter-argument that the opposition is exercising its right of trying to turn a minority view into the majority view. Ultimately, if in the government's view the opposition proves unduly obstructive, the amount of time devoted to any stage can be limited by use of the closure, the guillotine or other procedural devices. In any case the government and the opposition may informally agree on a timetable. In either event it will mean that some clauses of the bill will not be discussed at all or will be inadequately discussed.

To some extent it is a problem of time, although the House of Lords provides a means by which clauses inadequately dealt with in the Commons can be reviewed. But to provide more time in the Commons would not necessarily ensure adequate scrutiny because the essence of the problem is not time, but what it is used for. Standing committees are miniatures of the House of Commons not only in the sense that the parties are proportionately represented, but also in the procedural sense that the political confrontation of government versus opposition found on the floor of the House is repeated in standing committees. This is basically why Professor Griffith found a small number of bills occupied a large amount of time in the House of Commons and *vice versa*; bills over which the parties are divided tend to take longer more because the parties are divided than because of the complexities of the bills involved. Of course, the bills which take the longest are usually complex bills over which the parties are divided. It is not that the details of bills are entirely neglected, but once political solidarity rears its head detail is liable to be neglected.

Proposed remedies for this state of affairs are legion and we consider some of these later. What needs stressing at this point is that the only expertise that can normally be brought to bear in the parliamentary stage of the legislative process comes either from the ministers (aided by their civil servants) who are responsible for presenting the proposals, or from backbench MPs, some of whom may have an interest in and a knowledge of the matter under consideration. The expertise of ministers and civil servants, however, is not concerned with testing or scrutinising the details of legislation and the expertise of backbench MPs, valuable as it often is, is entirely fortuitous, arising not from the need to examine a particular piece of legislation but from the composition of the House of Commons. Thus even at the committee stage, whether it is taken in standing committee or in committee of the whole House, pressure groups and any other outside interests do not have direct access to the parliamentary stage of the legislative process. It is in fact procedurally possible for the committee stage of a bill to be taken by a *select* committee of the House of Commons and, unlike standing committees, select committees usually have the power to hear witnesses and receive written evidence. Governments, however, knowing that select committees tend to exhibit an independence largely absent in standing committees, rarely use this procedure. In the 1979–83 Parliament, however, the practice of appointing special standing committees, which are empowered to take oral and written evidence on bills referred to them, followed by the normal clause by clause examination, was introduced. In the event the government was reluctant to use them for most of its legislation and only five bills were dealt with in this way.

What many observers have regarded as a more hopeful sign in the past decade or more is a growing sign of independence amongst backbenchers, especially the government's own supporters, regardless of which party is in power. The Conservative Government of 1970–74 suffered six defeats on the floor of the House of Commons in four years of office, compared with a mere eleven defeats for governments of both major parties in the twenty-five years between 1945 and 1970. Between 1974 and 1979 the pace quickened, mainly, of course, because the Labour Government was in a minority situation for much of the time, but no less than twenty-three of the fifty-nine defeats the government suffered were caused by loss of support amongst its own backbenchers. The number of defeats in standing committees dealing with legislation was even greater and caused mostly by rebellions by government backbenchers. The return to majority government in 1979 has reduced the number of government defeats, but backbench rebellions or the threat of them, often resulting in concessions by the government, have become a significant feature of parliamentary life.

It is far too glib an answer, not to say pious hope, to argue that the government will have consulted all relevant pressure groups and interested parties at the preparatory stage of legislation, and that activity by outside interests to influence legislation during its passage through Parliament is simply a sign that earlier consultations did not achieve mutual satisfaction. This may well be the case, and action at Westminster may be indicative of failure in Whitehall, but it may also indicate a more fundamental failure on the part of the government to consult outside interests; practice in this respect seems to vary not only from government to government, but from bill to bill. One of the lessons of the Rent Act of 1957, on which consultation had been minimal, was that legislation based on inadequate information is likely to prove effective more by luck than judgment, and neither favoured the 1957 Act. The Labour Party had apparently learned this lesson, for it did consult widely among pressure groups over the 1965 Rent Act, and yet almost simultaneously forgot the lesson in preparing the Leasehold Reform Act of 1967. This might matter little were it not for the fact that once a government has committed itself publicly to certain proposals it is usually extremely reluctant to modify them in any significant way, so that unless prior consultation, shrewd guesswork or sheer good fortune (or some combination of these) have met the objections of outside interests and expert advice, then any errors of judgment are likely to be enshrined in the resulting Act of Parliament. Moreover, some groups may be so opposed to a policy that either the government sees little point in consulting them, or the groups themselves may refuse all offers of consultation as a means of protest, as the trade unions did in the face of Conservative industrial relations legislation in 1970–71 and again after 1979.

Parliament and scrutiny
Apart from its role in the legislative process, Parliament has other means by which it can scrutinise the activities and policies of the executive. Ministers can be interrogated at Question Time, infor-

mation can be extracted through questions for written answer, and almost anything can be debated. Used skilfully, each of these devices is a powerful parliamentary weapon. The doctrine of ministerial responsibility makes them so, not because Parliament may ultimately force the resignation of the government or an individual minister, but because ministers accept that they must answer parliamentary questions and defend their actions and policies in Parliament. It is an ill-advised minister who seeks to evade questions or who does not take a debate seriously, and many a ministerial reputation has been made and lost at Question Time or in debate. A skilful and determined backbencher can use parliamentary questions to extract much information or to conduct a campaign in favour of or against a particular policy, as did the late Sir Gerald Nabarro in the late '50s and early '60s over purchase tax anomalies, or, more recently, as Sir Philip Holland did against "quangos" or Tam Dalyell has over the sinking of the *Belgrano* in the Falklands conflict. In many respects, of course, the advantage lies with ministers, most notably in their access to relevant information and the backing they receive from their departments. Furthermore, far more questions are asked than can be orally answered, and above all the government controls the business of Parliament.

This last factor severely limits parliamentary scrutiny and yet the balance between executive and legislature is in certain respects a delicate one. Backbenchers, not least government backbenchers, have only to suspect that the government or a minister is trying to evade a question, ride roughshod over Parliament or, most of all, ignore it, and the balance can shift with alarming suddenness. Members of Parliament are political animals who, rightly or wrongly, tend to be very sensitive about the status of Parliament and the merest scent that Parliament has been "wronged" or that there is something that Parliament does not know that it should know, is sufficient to set the hunt in train.

In practice this means that Parliament, especially the House of Commons, is pretty effective in dealing with what may be termed the "political blow-up" – the sudden crisis or emergency, the unexpected development, such as the collapse of a company like Rolls-Royce in 1971 or Court Line in 1974, or the Turkish invasion of Cyprus in 1974 or, most dramatically in recent years, the Argentine invasion of the Falklands. Parliament tends to be effective – effective in the sense of making the government state its view and being able to question it – in these situations because it has the effective weapons of parliamentary questions, the emergency debate procedure under Standing Order 10, and the fact that it is difficult for the government to deny Parliament information on and the opportunity to discuss such matters.

What is more open to question is whether Parliament can effectively scrutinise the rest of the government's activities and policies. The most important means to this end, and the one on which the greatest hopes have been pinned by would-be reformers of Parliament, is the select committee. Select committees can be used for a variety of purposes. They may be used, but rarely are, to take the committee stage of bills. Similarly, they may be used to work out the detailed clauses of a bill which is not a matter of dispute between the parties. The Obscene Publications Bill, 1957 and the Armed Forces Bill, 1981 are examples of this use, but select committees are not used very often for this purpose. Select committees are used rather more frequently to investigate a particular matter and make recommendations – a recent example was the Select Committee on Members' Salaries. All these select committees have one thing in common: they are *ad hoc* committees and once they have completed their allotted tasks they cease to operate.

There are other select committees, however, which enjoy a more permanent existence, either because they are set up under the standing orders of the House of Commons or because they are reappointed each parliamentary session. Several of these committees are concerned with the internal working of the House of Commons and another is no longer of any great importance. All other select committees are directly concerned with the task of scrutinising the government. One, the Public Accounts Committee, is primarily a financial committee ranging over almost all areas of government responsibility. A further three have specially defined tasks: the Select Committee on Statutory Instruments (whose membership also operates as a joint committee with members of the House of Lords) examines delegated legislation to see that it is properly constituted and, where appropriate, presented to Parliament; there is a similar committee on European Secondary Legislation; and the Select Committee on the Parliamentary Commissioner (the "Ombudsman") examines the Parliamentary Commissioner's reports and maintains a watching brief over his work. The remaining fourteen select committees conduct investigations into almost the entire range of government responsibilities. They are the Select Committees on Agriculture; Defence; Education, Science and the Arts; Employment; Energy; the Environment; Foreign Affairs; Home Affairs; Industry and Trade; Scottish Affairs; the Social Services; Transport; the Treasury and the Civil Service; and Welsh Affairs. These committees are commonly known as the departmental select committees.

Select committees differ from standing committees in several important ways. First, select committees have traditionally been smaller than standing committees: with the exception of the Scottish Affairs Committee, which has thirteen members, the departmental select committees each have eleven members, whilst other select committees range between seven and sixteen. Standing committees may consist of as many as fifty members, but in recent years they have tended to be smaller, with twenty or so members.

Second, the membership of the more or less permanent select committees is fairly stable and each committee retains a core of members throughout a session and from one session to another. In contrast a fresh committee is set up to deal with each bill referred to standing committee and once the committee has dealt with the bill it is disbanded. This does not mean that MPs cannot sit on standing committees dealing with bills on which they have some specialised knowledge – this is one of the criteria for choosing MPs to serve on standing committees, but it does militate against legislation in a particular field always being dealt with by the same group of MPs and standing committees do not normally develop the committee identity commonly found in select committees which may override partisan points of view.

Third, select committees normally have the power "to send for persons, papers and records", whereas standing committees, other than special standing committees, may not hear witnesses or receive written evidence. This power enables select committees to question and secure written submissions from civil servants and outside experts, and to have access to certain government documents. It does not entitle committees to have access to all departmental documents, such as internal files and minutes or documents involving national security, and ministers cannot be required to appear before select committees, although ministers normally agree to appear. This power also allows outside organisations and individuals to submit evidence to select committees, although it is for the committee concerned to decide whether it wishes to hear oral evidence from any organisation or individual.

Fourth, select committees may have expert or specialist advisers to assist them in their investigations. In most cases such advisers are employed on an *ad hoc* basis to assist with particular investigations. The number of specialist advisers to select committees has increased considerably in recent years: between 1966 and 1972 twenty-eight advisers were appointed, but in the 1979–83 Parliament the fourteen departmental committees appointed no fewer than 171 specialist advisers and seven full-time research staff. The Public Accounts Committee (PAC), however, has the permanent assistance of the Comptroller and Auditor General, who has a staff of nearly nine hundred. The Comptroller and his staff, some of whom work in government departments, audit departmental accounts and draw to the Committee's attention any evidence of inefficiency and waste, as well as any financial discrepancies (which in practice are rare). All committees, select and standing, also have the assistance of one or more Clerks of the House of Commons. The Clerks are primarily procedural advisers, but in practice they make the necessary arrangements for committee meetings and, in the case of select committees, may help to organise research and advise the committee (especially the chairman) on a wide range of matters extending far beyond procedure.

Fifth, select committees, unlike standing committees, are miniatures of the House of Commons only in that their membership is in proportion to party representation in the House. The physical division of government supporters on one side of the room and opposition supporters on the other is replaced by a horseshoe seating arrangement; MPs do not stand but remain seated when participating in select committee proceedings; and the whole atmosphere is less formal and markedly less partisan than in standing committees. The chairman of a standing committee acts as Speaker of the committee and maintains a strict neutrality between the parties, whereas a select committee chairman plays a full part in the proceedings and usually leads the questioning of witnesses. By convention the chairmen of the Public Accounts Committee, and the Select Committees on Statutory Instruments, European Legislation, and the Parliamentary Commissioner are members of the opposition; and, since the 1983 election, five of the fourteen departmental select committee chairmen have been opposition MPs.

Investigation by select committee is undoubtedly an effective method of scrutinising the activities and policies of the executive. For the most part select committees are able to choose the matters for inquiry freely, although there have been clashes between committees and governments from time to time. The government can also limit a committee investigation by refusing certain information, usually on the grounds that it is not in the public interest to do so, but it is not practical politics to use this device too frequently or indiscriminately. Understandably, one of the most effective committees, given the assistance of the Comptroller and his staff, is the Public Accounts Committee, which was responsible, for example, for drawing attention in 1964 and 1965 to the excessive profits made by Ferranti on the Bloodhound missile and by Bristol-Siddeley on the overhaul of aero-engines. In both cases the firms repaid considerable sums to the Exchequer and changes were made in the methods of government contracting. More recently the PAC has produced important reports on strengthening parliamentary control of expenditure, leading to the passing of the National Audit Act, 1983, on the dispensing of drugs in the National Health Service in the 1982–83 session and of the enforcement powers of the Inland Revenue and Customs and Excise in 1983–84.

Other select committees have also proved effective in influencing policies or the course of events. The former Estimates Committee, for instance, produced a report in 1958 which led to the appointment of the Plowden Committee on the Control of Public Expenditure and the "forward-look" system of public expenditure by which an annual White Paper projects public expenditure several years ahead. The Estimates Committee was also responsible for a report in 1965 which resulted in the setting up of the Fulton Committee on the Civil Service, which led to important changes in civil service recruitment, training and organisation. The departmental committees set up in 1979 have also been having an impact. For example, in the 1979–83 Parliament the Home Affairs Committee played an important role in bringing about a change in the "sus" law – the power of the police to arrest persons on suspicion that they might intend to commit a crime; the establishment of the National Advisory Board for Public Sector

Higher Education owed much to a report of the Education Committee; and the Social Services Committee almost certainly influenced government policy on the arrangements for paying various social security benefits. The impact of many committee reports is less spectacular, but they have had a mundane though important effect in their fields. The committees provide a forum for the discussion of a wide variety of problems and policies and their reports should be seen as one of many inputs into the policy process. Moreover, many reports provide a wealth of information previously unavailable or difficult to obtain.

It is pertinent to ask, what lies beyond effective scrutiny? Does the government have to take any notice of select committee reports? The number of reports submitted by select committees in a parliamentary session of normal length can vary considerably, but it is usually between forty and fifty, of which only one or two will be debated. As a measure of influence; however, such figures are of little significance, since it is just as misleading to assume that because a report has been debated it has been influential, as it is to assume that the absence of a debate denotes absence of influence. The government does in fact formally reply to most select committee recommendations, although some recommendations may be directed not at the government but at other organisations or persons, such as local authorities or the members of a particular profession, whilst some merely urge that the government should keep a matter under review. Furthermore, many of the departmental committees have begun the develop the practice of later following up what has happened to recommendations made in earlier reports.

The short answer to the question is that the government does not have to take any notice of committee reports, but then neither does the House of Commons, even in theory. Select committees report to the House of Commons and procedurally the House may debate or ignore a report, accept it or reject it. Select committees do not decide, they recommend. All too often it is assumed that if the government ignores or rejects a committee's report, then the government is wrong and the committee is right, but there is another side to the coin.

Should Parliament decide?

We know well enough the answer to the question, can Parliament decide? The answer is no, except on private members' bills and on those few matters which the parties are prepared to leave to a free vote. Of course, if no party has a majority in the House of Commons then Parliament can decide more and its influence may be increased considerably, but the initiative remains with the government. This was vividly illustrated between February and October 1974 and 1976 and 1979, when the then Labour Government lacked a majority, and was forced to make concessions on a number of matters, yet still succeeded in getting more than four-fifths of its legislation through the House of Commons. It can be and is argued that Parliament in general and MPs in particular are powerless in the face of the party machines, and that the government's control of the House of Commons is absolute. This, however, is to misconstrue the nature of party politics. Leaders neither control their parties nor are controlled by them: the relationship is infinitely more subtle. Party leaders must retain the support of their followers and therefore do not totally ignore their views; conversely, party supporters are fully aware that the power of the party (in government or in opposition) depends ultimately on parliamentary cohesion. An examination of the division lists suggests that the influence of MPs is negligible, but the division lists are only one indication of backbench activity and the topic of a particular division may already have been subject to backbench influence in that leaders shape policy partly in anticipation of the reactions of their supporters. Backbench rebellions in the lobbies are often evidence of failure to influence policy at an *earlier* stage rather than evidence that backbench influence is negligible. Debates, parliamentary questions, private members' bills, committee reports, motions signed by MPs, party meetings – all parliamentary activity contributes to the noisy environment in which governments exist and politics operates.

Parliament, however, is only one source of noise, and a multifarious one at that. Outside Parliament the pressure groups and organised and unorganised opinion add their contribution. Sometimes it is possible to isolate a single sound which has influenced the government most, but more often there is a confusion of sound. Furthermore, it is not only the sounds which are heeded that may be important, but also those which are not. Some may have been heard and not heeded, others may not have reached the ears of the government, and this has led to various proposals for more "open government", especially through parliamentary reform.

A great deal of attention has inevitably been focused on the use of select committees. Reformers proposed that there should be a comprehensive system of select committees covering all areas of governmental responsibility, and some concessions were made to that point of view with the establishment of select committees from 1966 onwards in such areas as science and technology, education, agriculture, overseas aid, race relations, and Scottish affairs. These committees did not constitute a committee *system*, however, but merely a series of committees in particular areas. Furthermore, some of the committees had somewhat chequered careers and the experiment satisfied neither the proponents nor the opponents of what became known as specialised committees.

In 1971 several of the specialised committees were abolished, together with the Estimates Committee, and the Select Committee on Expenditure was established. The new committee was first and foremost a new style Estimates Committee with more powers to examine the policies implied in the annual estimates, but it also incorporated through its subcommittees (Public Expenditure, Defence and External Affairs, Trade and Industry, Education and the Arts, Employment and Social Services, Environment and the Home Office) some of the areas covered by the defunct specialised committees and, more importantly, extended its activities to others not previously covered. However, the Expenditure Committee disappointed some advocates of a specialised and comprehensive committee system because it did not dramatically transform the relationship between the executive and the legislature.

This dissatisfaction led to the appointment of a Select Committee on Procedure in 1977–78 which reported in favour of replacing the Expenditure Committee with a comprehensive select committee system covering all government departments and allowing standing committees to hold evidence-taking sessions. In 1979 the newly-elected Conservative Government accepted the proposal regarding select committees and the Expenditure Committee was replaced by the present fourteen departmental select committees.

The proposal that standing committees should be able to take evidence on the committee stage of bills found less favour, but it has its attractions, especially for those who fear that adoption of the full select committee procedure would lead to consensus politics in which the real differences between government and opposition would be papered over by a veneer of compromise. Pressure groups which had been consulted by the government in the privacy of Whitehall would be able to state their cases *publicly*, and in time might be expected to do so. Those groups which had not been consulted, together with any interested parties, would have an opportunity of putting their point of view. As for MPs, they would be more involved in the legislative process and better able to scrutinise bills.

There are also those who would like to see MPs involved in the preparatory stage of the legislative process, either by creating pre-legislation committees in Parliament or by appointing MPs to royal commissions, advisory committees and other bodies which may recommend legislative action to the government. Both are possible and used to some extent. Prelegislation committees, in the form of select committees, have been used for bills such as the Obscene Publications Bill 1957 and the Armed Forces Bill 1981, as we have already noted, but governments have shown little enthusiasm beyond this and show no inclination to return to the practice, fairly wide-spread in the nineteenth century, of using select committees to conduct major inquiries and in some cases to propose draft legislation. MPs are appointed to various advisory bodies outside Parliament, but not in any regular way, nor in great numbers.

As far as prelegislation committees are concerned there are problems of deciding which subjects should be so treated. With the exception of social issues such as abortion, homosexuality and divorce, governments, regardless of their political complexion, tend to regard the whole of society as their domain and insist on retaining the legislative initiative. This is understandable on issues close to the government's ideological heart, but hardly true of all issues. Just as some consultation could be brought into the open by allowing evidence to be heard on bills, so on some issues it could be brought more into the open by allowing committees to probe, inquire and make recommendations for legislation. Of course, consultation, like diplomacy, cannot be successfully conducted entirely in the market-place; the flexibility encouraged by secret negotiation may be lost, positions may harden, and compromise become more difficult, but no one is suggesting that secrecy be abandoned, merely that it should be balanced by more openness. The appointment of MPs to advisory bodies is a rather different matter. It is not a question of attempting to involve Parliament in any formal way in the preparatory stage of policy, but of trying to introduce in a more systematic way an element of parliamentary experience into these bodies and experience of the problems of policy-making among MPs.

Proposals to establish a comprehensive system of select committees, to make use of prelegislation committees and to involve MPs in the work of advisory bodies have all met with the objection that they would entail a derogation of ministerial responsibility on the grounds that someone other than the minister would be making decisions on matters for which the minister was responsible to Parliament. This objection does not bear examination. Advisory bodies outside Parliament are *advisory* bodies: they can decide nothing except what to recommend, so why should the appointment of MPs to serve on them make governments any more or less inclined to accept their advice? As for parliamentary committees – standing committees, select committees, prelegislation committees – all committees are by definition creatures of Parliament and may do no more than make recommendations to the body that appointed them. Certainly, the experience of the departmental committees since 1979 does not appear to have undermined ministerial responsibility, although some observers have been critical of the way in which civil servants have been identified with particular policies through giving evidence to the committees. Such fears are probably exaggerated, however, so long as the minister continues to accept ultimate responsibility for policy. As long as the government retains control of Parliament the fate of those recommendations is in the hands of the government. Of course, if the government loses control of Parliament or finds its control weakened by being in a minority situation, it will be a different story, but it will be a different story whether committees exist or not.

The real obstacles to allowing Parliament a greater involvement in the scrutiny of the executive and the formulation of policy are threefold. First, governments simply find it easier that way. Governments do not want to lay themselves open to wider and possibly more effective scrutiny, thus making life potentially more difficult; governments do not want to risk making things easier for their opponents to criticise; in short, governments do not want to make it more difficult to govern. Sympathy with this point of view is likely to be found at least in the major opposition party, which will not only normally have had the experience of government in the past, but hopes to enjoy it again and sees such proposals from the point of view of a *potential* government.

Second, governments do not wish to share the exercise of power any more widely than absolutely necessary. Any sharing of power is a dimunition of power, a limit on the government, and a curbing of its ability to decide. Once again this point of view is likely to be shared by the main opposition party. Third, and arising in part out of the second point, parties in power (and those who aspire to power) do not wish to see their ability to implement their policies diminished. They fear the dilution of their principles and the tainting of party policies with compromise.

It is only fair to point out that concessions to greater parliamentary scrutiny have been made, notably in the creation the Select Committee of Nationalised Industries in the 1950s and the succession of specialised select committees culminating in the departmental committees of 1979. These may be dismissed as sops to the reformers, yet in allowing these committees to be set up and, in most cases, to continue, successive governments have made life more difficult for themselves, widened the scope of scrutiny, in a sense shared power, and risked the dilution of their principles, no matter how small the extent.

It should also be acknowledged that the objections that governments, all governments, have to these proposals are not without foundation. Britain has a long-standing tradition and experience of government by a party with a majority in the House of Commons in which periods of minority government have been fairly short, and coalitions have usually been of limited duration for specific purposes, such as the prosecution of war. Parties have not been used to sharing power with each other nor with Parliament. On the contrary, Parliament has been the means by which parties have been able to implement their policies. Finally, regardless of the extent to which parties have been the vehicles of the ambitions of individual politicians, political parties in Britain are more important as the vehicles of particular sets of ideas and values. Most people do not belong to and work for a particular party because they are supporters of Margaret Thatcher, Neil Kinnock, David Steel or David Owen, or some other party leader, but because they support the sort of policies put forward by the Conservative, Labour, Liberal, Social Democratic or some other party.

It is not however a division between government and Parliament, nor between frontbenchers and backbenchers, for MPs are divided in their views, as four statements made in Granada Television's programme *The State of the Nation*, shown in July 1973, illustrate:

> *Mr John Mackintosh:* . . . I believe that as a Parliament we would be far more effective if we could elucidate the facts, we could investigate the Executive, we could find out the prior deals and get in on the formative stage of legislation.
>
> *Rt Hon. Enoch Powell:* . . . We must in order to do our business be uninvolved. We are not participating in government, we are not experts. . . . We have our own expertise, and our expertise is as politicians and would-be Ministers facing other politicians and actual Ministers, to strike our finger upon the places where it hurts, or upon the places where the great clash of politics is going to take place, and fight it out. We can only do that through debate, we can only do that on the Floor of the Chamber.
>
> *Rt Hon. Edward du Cann:* . . . a serious examination of huge programmes . . . cannot be achieved alone by general debate, nor can we compare alternatives effectively, road against rail, let us say, more money on preventive medicine or on treatment. We cannot compare alternatives alone by general debate . . . there is a catalogue of detailed work . . . exposing difficulties, exposing problems, getting the information for Members of Parliament.
>
> *Mr Michael Foot:* . . . what we are concerned about is maintaining the party battle, the conflict of clash of interest. And the real issues must come out into the House of Commons. All the remedies that are proposed . . . would reduce the party struggle, would reduce the clash of interests, would reduce the clash of politics generally. It would reduce it to a technical affair . . . [and] . . . plunge us into the kind of coalition methods which would destroy the real clash and battle of democracy in this country.[3]

In a sense this argument is about the meaning of the term "parliamentary control". Does it mean enforcing political accountability of the government to Parliament or detailed scrutiny of the government by Parliament? It can be argued that it means both and that detailed scrutiny is an effective means of enforcing political accountability, so that the argument appears to be one of means rather than ends. This appears so because the broad division is between those who believe that the focus of parliamentary activity should be the chamber of the House of Commons and those who favour a comprehensive system of committees.

The chamber advocates or "floor-men" argue that between elections it is Parliament's task to debate the political issues of the day, to continue the struggle between the rival parties, and to render the government accountable by forcing it to justify its policies in ideological, moral and philosophical terms and not in terms of cost-effectiveness and efficiency.

The "committee-men" argue that only committees with the power to receive evidence and question witnesses, including ministers and civil servants, can give Parliament an effective means of finding out what the government has done, or intends to do, and why. Parliament as a whole, they argue, cannot hope to look at every government action, but more could be looked at by dividing the work among committees. The floor of the House is regarded as the place for debating issues rather than systematic detailed investigation.

Looked at as a means of securing some form of parliamentary control the views of the "floor-men" and the "committee men" are not mutually exclusive, but the argument relates to ends as well as means. The "floor-men" feel that the use of select committees leads to a form of consensus politics in which a committee view is likely to prevail over the party views which normally divide MPs. Consensus politics would blur the lines between the parties and their ideological and philosophical inclinations would be swallowed up in a managerial approach to politics. The "committee men" regard these views as exaggerated and misconceived and assert that while the parties in Parliament play their political games the government continues to govern largely unobserved, a situation governments prefer and which accounts for the general reluctance to create a comprehensive committee system. Committees, they argue, would provide information which could be used to enforce political accountability on the floor of the House of Commons.

In short, it is a case on the one hand of believing that principles are in danger of being submerged in committee conclaves and that debates in the chamber are in danger of being relegated to a position of minor importance; or, on the other, of believing that Parliament is becoming increasingly incapable of keeping a check on the government and that detailed committee investigations provide the best means of redressing the balance.

Whichever of these arguments is preferred, in neither case is it a question of Parliament being given the power of decision. Parliament would decide only where and when the government chose to allow, or in circumstances in which the government no longer controlled Parliament. To give Parliament the *right* to decide would involve a fundamental change in the political system. Such a change is unlikely, but its nature should be understood.

Under the present system the government has the initiative in making policy; it decides which policies shall be implemented and which shall not; it decides, for good or ill, the nation's priorities. If, however, the right to initiate and to decide were given, say, to parliamentary committees, or to some extent shared with them, this could only be at the expense of the powers of initiative and decision at present enjoyed by the government. The government's role as determinant of policy priorities and policy coordinator would be eliminated or reduced. If the functions of the executive were divided among or shared with parliamentary committees the deciding of priorities and the coordination of policies would become more difficult. Even assuming all committee decisions were subject to the approval of Parliament as a whole (or at least the negative control of being approved unless rejected within a specified period), this would remain a major problem, and would create a situation in which it would be easier to mobilise parliamentary opinion *against* something than *for* something, as the fate of many private members' bills demonstrates. Above all, Parliament's principal function of scrutinising the activities and policies of the executive would be seriously undermined, for if Parliament assumed any significant executive functions, who would scrutinise Parliament?

The real argument is not about whether Parliament should decide, but how it can best carry out its primary function of scrutinising the executive. Parliamentary government does not mean government *by* Parliament but government *through* Parliament. Governments must eventually render themselves accountable to the people – to public opinion – at general elections, but between elections they are accountable to no one unless it is to Parliament. The political reality of accountability to Parliament, however, does not consist of ultimately sterile arguments over ministerial responsibility, but of publicly forcing the government to reveal, explain and justify its policies and actions.

6 Parliament and public opinion

What is public opinion?
We all have our opinions, yet others constantly take it upon themselves to tell us what we think. Politicians regard themselves as the
guardians and interpreters of public opinion; civil servants are
supposed to tell the politicians what the public will or will not stand
for; and the mass media – television, radio and the press – see
themselves as the voices of public opinion. The advent of public
opinion polls provided yet more grist for these particular mills and
yet seemed to offer the hope that some of the wilder claims of what
the public believed or did not believe might be curbed. Unfortunately
for the opinion polls, after successfully forecasting the result in each
general election between 1945 and 1966, their reputations became
tarnished in the election of 1970 and the two elections of 1974,
although they did better in 1979 and 1983. This only served to
confirm the views of those politicians and commentators who had
cast doubt on the accuracy of the polls, but who invariably contrived
to believe those polls which supported their view and reject those
which did not. Public opinion can therefore be a matter of conjecture,
of mere wishful thinking, as well as the obvious – what people think.
What a politician, civil servant or commentator believes to be public
opinion may bear little or no resemblance to what people really
believe, but for that particular politician, civil servant or commentator what he believes will be public opinion. This should not be dismissed as a cynical device for ignoring "real" public opinion, for
public opinion is less easily discerned than might at first be apparent.

What, for example, are the common sources of public opinion?
Where do politicians, civil servants and commentators get the
information which enables them to pronounce with such certainty

what the public thinks? For politicians in particular elections are the most obvious source of public opinion, not only general elections but the twenty to thirty by-elections that occur in a four or five year Parliament. Between elections the mass media are an obvious source, both through the hard news they disseminate and discussion of and comments on that news. The public may also directly express views by letters to the press and, more recently, by "phone-in" programmes on radio and television. Discussion programmes have also increased in number in recent years and it has become a frequent practice to invite members of the public to participate as studio audiences. Another important source, especially for politicians and journalists, is simply that of meeting people, whether at meetings (private or public), interviews, or just a casual exchange of views. Politicians in particular have also come to favour the "walkabout", especially at elections, as a means of bringing them into direct contact with public opinion, whilst most MPs, and some parliamentary candidates, also come into direct contact with the public through their "surgeries". And, of course, there are those much disdained, carefully watched devices, the opinion polls, which not only ask samples of the electorate how they will vote if there is a general election tomorrow, but what their views are on this matter or that. It is worth remembering that the politicians' disdain of opinion polls does not prevent them from using private polls to help them plan their political and electoral strategies and tactics.

It is often difficult, however, to say exactly what public opinion is on a particular matter, quite apart from the fact that it can change over time. For instance, no one would seriously argue that the writers of letters to *The Times* represent a microcosm of the nation, but it is doubtful whether all the letter-writers to all the newspapers put together do either. Similarly, we cannot be certain whether "phone-in" programmes or studio audience discussions give an accurate or distorted picture of public opinion. Do politicians and journalists get an accurate picture from meetings and "walkabouts"? All these sources can and do provide accurate glimpses of public opinion, but the accuracy of those glimpses often depends on the perceptions of the observer. Some observers, including many politicians, are highly skilled at discerning and divining public opinion, but the result is often highly impressionistic.

Elections and opinion polls are different to the extent that they are expressions rather than impressions of opinion, but they remain very much open to interpretation. How far, for example, was the result of the general election of February 1974 an expression of a desire for coalition government? An opinion poll taken before the election in January 1974 would suggest that it was: 64 per cent of the respondents said they wished to see a coalition of all parties, 29 per cent were against a coalition, and 7 per cent were "don't knows" (NOP, January 1974). The election results can tell us how many people voted for each party, which candidates were elected, and so on, but they cannot tell us why people voted the way they did. Did they vote for parties or candidates? How many voters saw the election as a choice between Heath and Wilson? How many voters consciously voted in a way calculated to bring about coalition government? The opinion poll tells us that in January 1974 more than three-fifths of a national sample of electors favoured a coalition, but it is an assumption that in February they tried to create a coalition situation. It is an assumption partly because an opinion poll is not a prediction of opinion or behaviour, but an expression of opinion at a particular time, and opinion may subsequently change; partly because the poll did not ask respondents if they intended to vote in such a way as to create a coalition situation; and partly because the electorate would require extremely detailed electoral information to know how they should vote in their respective constituencies in order to bring about a coalition situation.

Public opinion is a complex phenomenon. It is common to speak of public opinion favouring this or that, but in practice there is an infinite variety of "public opinion" on an infinite range of matters. The position may become clearer if we examine the main characteristics of public opinion.

Table 6.1 illustrates two important characteristics of public opinion. First, public opinion is usually divided between two or more points of view. In this case it was evenly divided, in that in 1976 40 per cent of the respondents were satisfied with the parliamentary system and 42 per cent were dissatisfied. Second, the table shows that an opinion may be held with varying degrees of intensity: in this case 6 per cent were "very strongly satisfied" and 17 per cent were "very strongly dissatisfied" with the parliamentary system. Conversely, 20 per cent were "not strongly satisfied" and 10 per cent were "not strongly dissatisfied".

Table 6.1   Satisfaction and dissatisfaction with the parliamentary system in Britain, 1976 (%)

Very strongly satisfied	6
Strongly satisfied	14
Not strongly satisfied	20
	—
Total satisfied	40
Not strongly dissatisfied	10
Strongly dissatisfied	15
Very strongly dissatisfied	17
	—
Total dissatisfied	42
Don't know	17
	—
Total	99

Source: Social Surveys (Gallup), August 1976. Very similar results were shown in a Gallup Poll in September 1968.

These two characteristics merely relate to one opinion, but two other important characteristics are concerned with the relationship of one opinion to another or between a whole range of opinions. The first of these is the relative importance or salience of two or more opinions to each other. This is illustrated by a series of polls between 1978 and 1984 which asked respondents which of the problems facing Britain they regarded as most urgent.

In 1978 over two-fifths of the respondents shown in Table 6.2 regarded unemployment as the most urgent problem facing Britain, with the cost of living and prices in second place. A year later, following the industrial disputes of "the winter of discontent", the cost of living and prices and strikes occupied the first two places, with unemployment edged into third place. In each subsequent year, however, as the number out of work increased, unemployment was regarded as the most urgent problem, challenged only by strikes in 1984, no doubt reflecting the prolonged miners' strike. Over the same period the cost of living and prices dwindled as inflation fell. It is also clear from Table 6.2 that, although there may be widespread or significant agreement as to what is important, there is not unanimity, so that

Table 6.2   Public opinion on the most urgent problems facing Britain

1978				% thinking it the most urgent problem Year			
Problem	1978	1979	1980	1981	1982	1983	1984
Unemployment	43	18	64	77	79	73	53
Cost of living & prices	24	25	18	8	5	—	3
Other economic problems	6	6	5	3	2	3	—
Strikes	5	20	2	—	3	3	32
Law and order	4	—	1	2	2	3	2
Immigration	2	—	—	—	—	—	—
Other	13	21	11	10	8	12	7
Defence	—	—	—	—	—	4	2
Ireland	—	6	—	—	—	—	—
Don't know	3	4	1	1	1	2	1

Source: Social Surveys (Gallup), September 1978–September 1984.
Note: The figures do not always total 100 because of rounding.

what is important to one individual is less important or unimportant to another.

This may lead to a situation in which an individual must, consciously or otherwise, effectively choose between two or more of his opinions: the dilemma of the voter who prefers Conservative handling of foreign affairs, Labour's handling of industrial relations, and finds the Liberal-SDP Alliance candidate the most attractive of three standing in his constituency does not need elaboration. Yet most voters do make a choice, consciously or unconsciously, rationally or irrationally, and for many that choice is influenced by what is important to them, by the salience of their opinions.

Salience may offer an explanation for the second characteristic concerned with the relationship between opinions, consistency – the extent to which holding one opinion is consistent with holding another. For many years, for example, opinion polls have found majorities against further nationalisation, but this has not prevented the return of Labour governments pledged to further nationalisation, although it certainly contributed to the late Hugh Gaitskell's attempt to reduce the Labour Party's commitment to public owner-ship. Clearly some voters who oppose further nationalisation must have voted Labour. It is likely that some, though not all, of these voters were aware of Labour's nationalisation policies, but none-theless preferred a Labour government. Any inconsistency may therefore be more apparent than real.

Lack of information is by no means a bar to expressing an opinion, but it is important to appreciate that there are on many issues a high proportion of "don't knows", some of whom may be genuinely undecided in their opinions, whereas others may simply feel that they lack sufficient information to express an opinion.

This phenomenon is illustrated in Table 6.3, which summarises the proportions of "don't knows" in a series of opinion polls in which respondents were asked whether they were satisfied or dissatisfied with various government policies. Apart from the poll conducted in October 1979 the average proportion of "don't knows" was between 11 and 16 per cent, but they ranged from as low as 4 per cent to as high as 38 per cent. The lowest proportion of "don't knows" in every year except one, when it was the second lowest, was on the cost of living and prices and the highest proportion in every year except one was on roads. The rank order of policies suggests that respondents were more willing to express views on policy areas that were likely to cause them concern and about which they were likely to know something. The issues lower down the rank order were also issues which might cause concern, but they tended to be issues on which respondents might feel less well-informed and therefore less able to express an opinion.

Table 6.3 further suggests that the willingness to express opinions varies over time. The first poll cited in the table (October 1978) was taken after more than four-and-a-half years of Labour govern-ment and the seventh (October 1984) after five-and-a-half years of Conservative government: both show similar results. The poll of October 1979, however, followed five months after a change of government and showed a clear increase in the proportion of "don't knows". The decline in the proportion of "don't knows" can be illustrated more dramatically by examining opinions on party leaders. For example, in February 1975, shortly after she became Leader of the Conservative Party, 41 per cent of respondents were "don't knows" in a poll asking them whether they were satisfied or

Table 6.3   Proportions of "don't knows" on satisfaction and dissatisfaction with government policies, 1978–84

A. Average and range of proportions of "don't knows" %	Oct. 1978	Oct. 1979	Dec. 1980	Dec. 1981	Sept. 1982	Oct. 1983	Oct. 1984
Mean	16.2	19.4	12.5	11.9	11.6	12.4	13.1
Median	15	18	12	11	10.5	11	12.5
Range	7–29	9–38	5–23	4–22	4–22	6–22	5–21

B.   Rank order of policies
1. Cost of living and prices (lowest proportion of "don't knows").
2. National Health Service
3. Law and order
4. Strikes and labour relations
5. Education
6. Taxation
7. Full employment
8. Old age pensions
9. Economic and financial affairs generally
10. Defence and armaments
11. Housing
12. The Common Market
13. Immigration
14. Roads (highest proportion of "don't knows")

Source: Social Surveys (Gallup), October 1978–October 1984.

dissatisfied with Mrs Thatcher's leadership; by November 1975 the proportion had fallen to 25 per cent. Similarly, in November 1983, shortly after he became Labour Leader, the proportion of "don't knows" on the same question about Neil Kinnock was 50 per cent; by September 1984 it had fallen to 26 per cent (National Opinion Polls). While it is not surprising that the proportions of "don't knows" should rise after a new government takes office, it is striking after several years in office that it is not unusual to find as many as 20 per cent of the respondents among the "don't knows" on important policy areas.

This means that there are policies on which significant proportions of the public may have no opinion. Of course, it can be argued that it is the job of politicians to articulate and elicit public opinion, and this is precisely what they seek to do on many issues, particularly in election campaigns. There is opinion poll evidence that in some instances the proportion of "don't knows" falls on issues that the politicians and the mass media bring to the attention of the public, especially where the parties give a clear lead to their supporters. In other cases the reverse happens, notably where one point of view is initially given a great deal of publicity, but as counterarguments receive more attention the proportion of "don't knows" may increase in response to the cross-pressures thus created and the division of opinion may alter. There is also a limit to what the politicians and the media can bring to the public's attention and the media can only interest themselves in a limited amount of news, and therefore issues, at any one time. Thus the politicians and the media can articulate public opinion and the opinion polls can provide a great deal of information about public opinion, but between them they can only tap a small part of it at any one time. Much is therefore left to the conjecture, intuition and judgment of politicians and commentators, upon their ability to "read" the public mind. Highly developed as this ability may be in many politicians and commentators, it is as well to remember that it remains an art rather than a science.

Public opinion is not an immutable phenomenon; it is likely to change in response to changing circumstances. It can be very stable, but it can also be highly volatile and today's majority may be tomorrow's minority. More often than not there is no way of knowing whether those expressing opinions are well-informed or not, how much consideration has been given to the matter, how strongly they feel about it, nor how important it is to them. Moreover, although the public is often treated as a single entity, in reality it is a myriad of groups and interests. Public opinion is not merely a national phenomenon, but may be based on region, locality, occupation, class, age, sex, education, membership of organisations, on this interest or that. Similarly there are national issues, local issues, sectional issues, moral issues, technical issues. The result is not the unified public opinion of political rhetoric, but a potentially infinite number of public opinions.

Public opinion and policy

The impact of public opinion on policy is easy to illustrate but difficult to assess. In part this is because so many decisions are made
behind closed doors, but it is also due to the complex nature of
public opinion itself. Furthermore, the relationship is not a simple
causal one of public opinion making itself known and the politicians
reacting accordingly. The situation is often reversed: the politicians
act and the public reacts.

There are examples of Parliament or the government responding
to public opinion, but there are also examples of public opinion
clearly being flouted. Probably the most familiar case of the latter is
Parliament's abolition of the death penalty for murder in 1965, in
spite of the fact that opinion polls had for years consistently shown
substantial majorities against abolition. Moreover, MPs have
continued to defy public opinion by voting on several occasions
against the reintroduction of the death penalty for specific types of
murder or for terrorist offences. Another example is the Conservative
Government's banning of trade unions at GCHQ (the government
communications centre), which, according to a Gallup Poll, was
regarded as unjustified by 62 per cent of its respondents (Social
Surveys (Gallup), February 1984). Mrs Thatcher's Government has
also been unmoved by opinion polls repeatedly showing majorities
against the siting of cruise missiles in Britain.

The case of British entry into the Common Market is more
complex. In the mid-1960s Gallup found absolute majorities in
favour of British entry, but in April 1967 there was only a relative
majority of 43 per cent in favour, and in May 1967 a relative majority
of 41 per cent against. For a year opinion swayed to and fro, but
from June 1968 relative majorities, and between March 1970 and
June 1971 absolute majorities, against were recorded. Opinion then
began to waver again, although there was usually a relative majority
against entry, until in January 1973, when British entry became a
fact, 38 per cent of Gallup's respondents thought it was right for
Britain to join the Common Market, 36 per cent thought it was
wrong, and 26 per cent did not know (Social Surveys, 1965–73). The
Common Market example differs from the others in that opinion
varied considerably over time and for much of the time there were
only relative majorities for or against entry and opinion was often

fairly evenly balanced, whereas the three earlier examples were un-equivocal expressions of public opinion. Nonetheless, it can still be argued that if entry into the Common Market was something less than the flouting of public opinion, it was hardly in accord with it. The endorsement of British membership in 1975 did not alter this; it was a reflection of a further change in public opinion.

The Immigration Acts of 1962 and 1968 are examples of govern-ments being influenced directly by public opinion. In 1962 the Conservative Government, aware of growing public concern over Britain's immigrant population, passed an Immigration Act which was bitterly opposed by the Labour Party. On assuming office in 1964, however, after a general election in which the immigration issues had clearly been important in a number of constituencies, Labour not only found it politically judicious to retain the act, but actually strengthened immigration controls when faced with the influx of Kenyan Asians in 1968 and both parties remain very sensitive to public opinion an immigration.

The saga of the third London airport is a further example of public influence playing its part, but it also illustrates the way in which public feeling can be ignored for a long period. In the early 1960s both major parties agreed that the third London airport should be built at Stansted in Essex, despite some strong local opposition. The change of government in 1964 therefore did nothing to help those who opposed the choice of Stansted. In fact it was not until a change of minister occurred in 1967 that the Stansted pro-testers made any significant progress. The Roskill Commission was appointed to consider several possible sites, including Stansted, but its terms of reference made it likely that Stansted would not be recommended. This proved to be the case and the commission recommended Cublington in Buckinghamshire, but the residents of Cublington had other ideas and campaigned vigorously for the rejection of the Roskill Report. Fortune was on their side, for the Conservatives, who were now in office favoured Maplin Sands off the coast of Essex for the site of the third London airport, and so Maplin became the choice. Inevitably this led to an anti-Maplin group, whose chances of success seemed small so long as the Con-servatives remained in office, but the return of Labour in February 1974 came to their rescue and, ironically, the wheel has come almost full circle in that a more limited development is now proposed at Stansted.

There is also little doubt that public opinion played its part in persuading the government to retreat on imposing charges on students' parents for university tuition fees late in 1984 and in reversing its decision early in 1985 not to arrange any official celebrations on the fortieth anniversary of VE Day, which fell later that year.

The relationship between public opinion and policy is not a simple one in which the government (or Parliament) ignores public opinion only when it thinks it can get away with it, and responds positively to public opinion only when it fears the consequences of defying it. Public opinion, in fact, can be a frail basis for a policy, as the recent history of trade union legislation illustrates. In 1969 opinion polls found substantial majorities in favour of the main proposals contained in Mrs Barbara Castle's White Paper *In Place of Strife*, but faced with an extremely hostile reaction from the trade unions and ultimately unsure of its parliamentary support, the Labour Government abandoned its proposed legislation. Public opinion, however, continued to support changes in trade union law and Gallup found only a quarter of its respondents against the Conservative Government's Industrial Relations Bill in 1971 and more than 50 per cent in favour (Social Surveys (Gallup), February and March 1971).

The example of the 1971 Industrial Relations Act is a reminder that on many issues it is possible and legitimate to speak of public opinion generally, but that simultaneously various groups in and sections of society will also hold opinions which may or may not coincide with general opinion. Whether general opinion or particular opinion will prevail, assuming there is a conflict, depends on a variety of factors. In setting up the National Health Service, for example, the Labour Government of 1945–50 needed the cooperation of doctors, dentists and other medical workers and was therefore prepared to negotiate to secure it, but in nationalising the railways, and the coal, gas, electricity and steel industries that same government were not similarly dependent on the owners and shareholders of those industries once they had been nationalised. Clearly the success of the Industrial Relations Act depended on at least a minimum of cooperation from the trade unions and, although the Conservative

Government was fully aware of opposition of the unions to the Act, it hoped that most unions would cooperate to the extent of registering under the act and recognising the Industrial Relations Court. Various incentives were included in the Act to encourage such cooperation and the government hoped that in time the unions would cooperate more fully. What the government did not foresee is that the TUC would lead its members in a policy of non-cooperation, encouraged in part by the knowledge that the Labour Party was pledged to repeal the Act if it were returned to power. On the other hand, the trade unions have been less successful in resisting the step by step industrial relations policy pursued by the Conservatives following their return to power in 1979. Continuing high levels of unemployment, divisions amongst the unions themselves and a Labour Party further weakened by a second election defeat in 1983 have combined to strengthen the Conservative Government's hand.

Much also depends on the determination of the government to pursue particular policies: the Conservative Government elected in 1970 was determined to pass an Industrial Relations Act; its Labour successor was equally determined to repeal it. To varying degrees political parties adhere to particular values or ideologies which lead them to propose policies consistent with those values or ideologies. In broad terms the Conservative Party sees itself as the party of free enterprise, freedom of the individual, and the limitation of state intervention; the Labour Party sees itself as the party of socialism, equality, and more extensive state intervention. Similarly, both parties attract support disproportionately from different sections of society. It is not therefore surprising that both parties pursue policies which reflect their respective ideological stances and their differing sources of support. This can be seen in housing policy: the Conservative Party places greater emphasis on policies which help and encourage owner-occupation, whereas the Labour Party lays greater stress on council or municipal housing; the Conservatives' 1957 Rent Act and 1971 Housing Finance Act were designed to allow rents to rise closer to a free market level, whereas Labour's 1965 Rent Act and post 1974 policy were designed to control and limit rents; and the Conservative policy of allowing council tenants to purchase their rented houses contrasts with Labour's policy of allowing leaseholders to purchase the properties they lease. Similarly, Conservative policies of the denationalisation or privatisation of various state-owned industries contrasts with Labour's continued commitment to public ownership. In some cases policies may be pursued in spite of, rather than because of public opinion: where party ideology looms largest, public opinion may loom least.

Whatever may divide the parties ideologically, there has been a tendency in recent years for governments to pay more attention to public opinion. In fact, during the Second World War the government employed a survey organisation, Mass Observation, to assess the impact of the war on the civilian population and in particular to measure the effectiveness of government propaganda. For a number of years governments have had the assistance of the Social Surveys Division of the Office of Population Censuses and Surveys, which among other things conducts opinion surveys on behalf of the government. More significantly, a number of commissions and committees have made use of attitude surveys as part of their investigations. For example, the Maud Committee on the Management of Local Government (in 1964), the Committee on Privacy (in 1971), the Royal Commission on the Constitution (in 1971), the Boyle Committee on the pay of ministers and MPs (also in 1971) and the Peacock Committee on the financing of the BBC (in 1985), all had surveys of public opinion conducted on their behalf. But these cases illustrate the normal role that public opinion plays in politics generally. Public opinion is not the only factor in the determination or recommending of policy, nor is it necessarily the most important.

In some cases information about public opinion may help the government in coming to a decision or an investigatory body in making its recommendation. The Commission on the Constitution, for instance, used the findings of its survey to support its rejection of independence for Wales and Scotland and for its rejection of a federal system. In other cases such surveys may provide useful background information, but little more. The survey conducted on behalf of the Top Salaries Review Body found widespread ignorance about how much MPs were paid, what expenses they were entitled to, what other assistance they received, and the amount of time they spent on their parliamentary work. The tendency was to overestimate members' salaries and considerably underestimate the expenses they had to meet out of their own pockets, and the amount of time they spent on parliamentary work. Most respondents therefore tended to think that MPs were either overpaid or received adequate remuneration. Even when respondents were informed of the actual remuneration of MPs, only a third thought them underpaid:[1] had public opinion prevailed MPs would not have received an increase in salary and expenses in 1972.

Public opinion can and does find expression in Parliament, but it is very much open to interpretation, for MPs regard themselves as *interpreters* of public opinion and to an important extent they choose the issues on which they will give voice to public opinion. On most issues supporters and opponents of various points of view will be found in the House of Commons and, for that matter, in the House of Lords, and there are procedural means by which these points of view can be expressed. Even so, they can hardly be regarded as the systematic expression of public opinion, however much they may be an accurate reflection of parliamentary opinion, which itself may often be open to doubt. On issues such as abortion or immigration public opinion finds effective expression in Parliament, but as a continuous reflection of public opinion Parliament is less than regular and far from systematic. On many issues, public opinion is simply not known or is the subject of conjecture, shrewd or otherwise. Governments (and in many cases the opposition parties as well) may consult various groups and interests, or these groups and interests may make their views known, but in most cases the public will not have been consulted in any systematic way. The obvious question now, of course, is should public opinion prevail? It is to this question that we now turn.

Public opinion and politics
Public opinion can be measured in various ways and there is no doubt that it could be measured more systematically and more extensively than it is at present. Public opinion in Britain is at present measured systematically at elections and by means of opinion polls. In addition the referendum has been finding favour in some quarters in recent years. It therefore seems appropriate to look at each of these devices in turn.

Elections are notoriously difficult to interpret as expressions of public opinion, but popular subjects of interpretation nonetheless. After a general election the leaders of the winning party invariably claim that the nation has given them and their party "a vote of confidence". Furthermore, they may also claim that they have received a mandate from the people to carry out certain policies presented to the electorate in the party manifesto or during the campaign. By-election and local government election results are variously hailed as evidence of impending electoral triumph, doom or revival.

In practice, as we saw when we looked at general election results in Chapter 4, it is normally only a plurality, seldom a majority and least of all the overwhelming majority of the nation that could be described as giving the winning party "a vote of confidence". It is an assumption, however credible it may appear, that people vote for a party because they have confidence in it or its leaders. As for the mandate, few general elections are fought primarily on a single issue. The two general elections of 1910 were fought by the *Conservative and Liberal Parties* primarily on the constitutional issue of the primacy of the Commons over the Lords, but who can say categorically that it was this issue and this alone that determined the *voters'* choice? In their 1983 election manifesto the Conservatives clearly stated their intention, if re-elected, to abolish the Greater London Council and the metropolitan county councils. However, in 1984, when some of the necessary legislation was before Parliament, an opinion poll reported that 52 per cent of its respondents opposed abolition, but the government claimed it had a mandate for its policy (National Opinion Polls, May 1984). Who can say categorically how many voters supported any party in an election because of its policies rather than in spite of them? By-elections and local elections may well be precursors of what is to come, but as measurements of opinion they too suffer from the fact that we cannot know for certain from election results what influenced people in casting their votes.

This is not to say that reasonable inferences about public opinion cannot be made from election results. If the government suffers a series of by-election reverses or is defeated at a general election, it is reasonable to infer that a certain policy or policies (or absence of policies) account for the government's unpopularity, but *inference* it remains. Inferences can also be made from the distribution of party support, but we cannot be certain why support is distributed the way it is merely from election results.

Even so, the claims made by politicians about election results should not be dismissed as empty rhetoric. Elections probably do confer an important degree of legitimacy on governments and, even if the theory of the mandate is difficult to sustain in practice, it exists in the sense that some politicians and some voters probably believe in it.

Elections remain primarily an expression of the party preferences of the electors; they do not tell us what factors determined those preferences; nor do they tell us what public opinion is on any particular issue, much as they may remain rich sources of inference. Electoral studies have shown that some 37 per cent of the electorate always votes for the same party, regardless of its policies, its leaders and its candidates. These studies are based on sample surveys of electoral opinion, however, and it is these which enable us to test some of the inferences that are made about electoral behaviour, both generally and in respect of particular elections. It should not be forgotten that elections are not primarily intended to elicit public opinion on particular issues, but, given the way in which the electoral system works, to choose which party will govern for the next four or so years.

Surveys or opinion polls, on the other hand, are intended to elicit opinion and in practice provide us with the most accurate information that we have about public opinion. In recent years the polls have come under increasing criticism for getting election predictions "wrong", but this should not lead us to dismiss polls as worthless or spurious. Quite apart from the fact that their surveys of party support are reports of voting *intentions at the time the survey was conducted* and not predictions of how respondents will ultimately cast their votes, the opinion polls are invariably within the statistical limits of error of their samples. Furthermore, recent elections have been significantly affected by the level of turnout, differing turnouts and swings in different constituencies and parts of the country, and late changes of electoral opinion, all of which have contributed to the polls' difficulties. Nonetheless, whatever their sins the opinion polls are basically reliable "snapshots" of public opinion – "snapshots" because they are only strictly accurate at the time of the survey. In many cases, of course, opinion changes little, if at all, over quite long periods of time, but on other matters opinion may be fairly volatile or, especially where there is a significant proportion of "don't knows", remain fluid and uncertain. The polls may also be snapshots in another sense, in that they often deal with a series of *separate* issues, rather than a series of *related* issues. Academic surveys or polls usually seek to elicit views on a whole range of related issues, although it should be acknowledged that in the last few years opinion polls have conducted more surveys of this sort. It has also become the practice of a number of polling organisations to ask the same questions at regular and sometimes frequent intervals. Thus a picture of changing or static public opinion can be built up through a series of snapshots.

The post-war period has seen a mushrooming of polling organisations, so that our knowledge of public opinion on various issues has increased considerably. Evidence of public opinion on many of the major issues of domestic and foreign policy can be found in opinion poll reports, many of which are published through the mass media or in regular bulletins published by the polling organisations. But the polls can tap only a small area of public opinion at one time. Furthermore, it is the polls which choose the matters on which their respondents are questioned, although to an important extent events and current issues govern that choice. This means that the public can express their views through the polls, but for the most part cannot choose on *what* they express their views. Similarly, governments do not control the polling organisations in any way and therefore remain passive recipients of the information they produce, although polls are sometimes commissioned by the government and others are conducted by the Office of Population Censuses and Surveys. Finally, little attention is paid by the polls to the intensity, saliency and consistency of public opinion.

Some of the disadvantages of the use of opinion polls could be reduced or eliminated. More polls could be commissioned by the government on issues which are currently under consideration. Facilities or finance for polls could be made available to the opposition parties and to parliamentary committees. All such polls could be subjected to the scrutiny of a panel including experts on the relevant statistical theories and techniques, and persons with experience of questionnaire compilation and administration. Where appropriate, questions to test intensity, saliency and consistency could be included. Yet in all probability the innate suspicion that politicians and the public seem to have of opinion polls would remain. The politician appears to feel that the polls are usurping his prerogative of sensing and interpreting public opinion and the public appears to find it difficult to believe that a sample of, say, a thousand people, however carefully chosen, can accurately reflect the opinions of millions. As long as such suspicions remain it will be difficult to use opinion polls as the principal means by which public opinion is measured for the purposes of policy-making. They must remain grist for the mill; they cannot take over the functions of the mill itself.

There is one device, however, the referendum, which seems to avoid the problems of the opinion poll. A referendum does not depend on a sample of electors but is open to all electors. It is a device which is used and has been used in many countries. In Australia, for instance, referenda are used to accept or reject proposed constitutional amendments and the decision on entry into the EEC was made by referendum in Denmark, Ireland and Norway in 1972. In Switzerland, France and some states of the United States, however, the referendum is used more widely to allow the electorate to accept or reject specific policy proposals. In many cases the referendum is combined with another device, the initiative, which allows a specified proportion of the electorate to demand a referendum on a particular issue. A further variation is also found in a number of American states and municipalities in the form of the recall, by which elected office-holders (of whom there are many in American politics and administration) can be required to submit themselves to a further election during their term of office.

The referendum is intrinsically attractive, all the more so when combined with the initiative, in that it is a direct response to the plea, "Let the people decide". Yet it has attendant problems. Should a specified proportion of the electorate vote in order to make a referendum valid? Should approval of a proposal receive an absolute majority or is a relative majority of less than 51 per cent sufficient? If an absolute majority is required, is 51 per cent sufficient or should a majority of, say, two-thirds, be required? Who should decide the wording of the question or questions to be put to the electorate? Should the electorate be provided with information or statements supporting and opposing the proposal? Should the whole electorate be consulted on all proposals or should referenda on some proposals be limited to those directly affected?

Local referenda have been used in Britain – notably in Wales to decide whether public houses should be allowed to open on Sundays and a referendum was held in Northern Ireland in 1973 to test opinion on whether people wished the province to remain part of the United Kingdom or become part of the Republic of Ireland. Political parties have from time to time advocated the use of referenda for particular issues, but the referendum on British membership of the EEC in June 1975 was the first national use of the device. Then in 1978 referenda were held on the Labour Government's devolution proposals for Scotland and Wales, although they were confined to those parts of the country. The regular use of the referendum in Britain is opposed by the Conservative and Liberal Parties, and the Labour Party advocated its use only on the Common Market issue and has not committed itself to making it a permanent part of political machinery.

Research into the use of referenda and voting behaviour suggests that frequent resort to the ballot box tends to reduce turnout, which provides opponents of particular proposals with means of casting doubt on the validity of endorsement by referendum. Furthermore, if rules stipulating that turnout must be, say, at least 51 per cent and that an absolute majority is necessary for approval of a proposal, then again research evidence suggests that many proposals would not be accepted. Referenda are, in fact, widely regarded as conservative devices in which the electorate is likely to reject change rather than approve it, even where no conditions of level of turnout or size of majority are imposed.

Referenda also suffer from being associated with some authoritarian regimes, such as Hitler's Germany and, more recently, Greece under the "Colonels", which have used referenda to provide evidence of popular support. The way in which referenda can be used as tactical political weapons is further illustrated by their use in the Fifth French Republic. Under the constitution the President may submit various proposals to a referendum, and President de Gaulle used this power with considerable skill. Voters were asked two or more questions to which only a single answer was allowed, such as, "Are you satisfied with this Government and its economic policy?" De Gaulle invariably appeared on the state-controlled television the day before the referendum took place and made a personal appeal to the nation, not as a party leader, but as President of France, with the result that his opponents were denied the right of reply. The electorate, moreover, could not be certain what result a "non" vote would have. Would de Gaulle, who had brought prosperity and stability to France and restored French pride, regard the rejection of a proposal as a rejection of himself? Ironically, in 1969 de Gaulle did make it clear that if his proposals for regional reform and reform of the

Senate were rejected he would resign, and the electorate took him at his word and rejected them, whereupon de Gaulle promptly resigned as President.

There is no doubt that if the referendum were introduced in Britain as a regular part of the political machinery it would become a tactical political weapon. It might be that governments, if the choice were theirs alone, would use it sparingly, conscious of the fact that it is a double-edged weapon, but refusal to submit an issue to a referendum is itself a tactical weapon in the hands of the opposition. If the initiative were also introduced then a potentially powerful weapon would be placed in the hands of any group or interest which thought it could secure the support, however fleetingly, of a majority of the electorate. In all likelihood the referendum and the initiative would assist more those who wish to secure the rejection of a proposed policy than it would those who favour its acceptance.

Nonetheless, both devices would provide public opinion with opportunities to make itself felt in ways and to an extent which does not at present exist. Supposing it becomes technologically possible to dispense with the ballot box in its present form and provide each member of the electorate with access to a simple computer terminal, either in his own home, at work or in public locations, would this not facilitate widespread participation in the making of policy? Leaving aside questions of turnout and any conditions defining majority approval, such a development would take no account of the intensity, saliency or consistency of public opinion. The question "Should public opinion prevail?" needs to be considered in the light of another question: "*Whose* opinion should prevail?" Although we speak of public opinion, meaning the views of all adult members of society, it is also meaningful to speak of *expert* opinion (those who are acknowledged specialists in the area concerned), *informed* opinion (those who have some knowledge or acquaintance with the area concerned), and *affected* opinion (those who are directly affected by the matter). Indeed, when we speak of public opinion in practice we are sometimes referring to expert, informed or affected opinion. At present *public* opinion is but one of many factors which influence policy-making and neither government nor opposition, politician nor administrator lives by public opinion alone. Of course, it can be argued that political reality falls short of democracy if public opinion is not the decisive factor, but this is a matter for our final chapter.

7 Parliament and democracy

What is democracy?

There is no answer to this question that will satisfy everyone, for "democracy" is one of the most frequently used, ill-defined, and emotive words in the vocabulary of politics. Among modern régimes only the Fascist dictatorships have poured scorn on it, although even Hitler found the plebiscite a useful device. There is no more damning a political epithet than to describe a régime or opponent as "undemocratic". Is it possible that the single term "democracy" can encompass régimes as different as the Soviet Union, the United States, Tanzania, South Africa and Argentina? Yet most régimes in the world claim to be democratic and it would be unwise to dismiss their claims summarily merely because they do not conform to *our* idea of democracy, whatever it may be. Democracy is not a meaningless word that means all things to all men, but a *principle* which in practice means different things to different men.

It is misleading to regard democracy as a particular form of government: the existence of particular political institutions does not constitute democracy. Democracy is a principle which may find expression in a variety of institutions in many different ways and in many different forms. Democracy is *any* form of government which involves popular *consent* and popular *control*, but neither consent nor control need be absolute in that it is possible to conceive degrees of democracy. For example, a small organisation of, say, twenty members could take policy decisions by holding meetings of all twenty members at which no decision would be valid unless it received the consent of the members and each member would have the opportunity to state his point of view on any matter. It is a commonplace of discussions of democracy, however, to point out that this sort of

direct democracy in which all members of the organisation, association or society may participate on equal terms is possible in
small groups or in the Greek city state or the New England township,
but quite impractical in the mass societies of today. Some modifi-
cation is therefore necessary and various devices have been evolved
to facilitate the operation of democracy in a mass society. These
devices include various types of elections, the referendum, the initiative and, above all, the concept of *representative* democracy.
Through such devices some degree of popular consent and control
can be exercised. Thus it can be argued that if certain matters are
subject to approval by a referendum (whether as a result of the
initiative or not) or if people may elect representatives to a legislature, then to that extent the democratic principle is being operated
and to that extent democracy exists.

It is at this point that the real problems of defining democracy
begin, for it is a matter of opinion whether such devices really do
implement the democratic principle. There are those who argue that
democracy is a practical impossibility because it demands a level of
participation by the members of society which has seldom, if ever,
been achieved. One answer is to assume that people will participate
if they wish to, but this raises further problems. Can we assume that
non-participation indicates satisfaction or consent? Failure to
participate could equally well indicate disillusion, protest, alienation
or apathy. No doubt research could help resolve this problem, but it
would need to be continuing research and government by research is
hardly practicable.

Of course, it can be argued that there will always be some members
of society who are alienated or apathetic, but that provided a majority
of people participate in the political process democracy prevails.
But what is meant by "participation in the political process"? It may
be true that in Britain a majority of the electorate vote in general
elections, but in what other sense does a majority participate? A
majority read newspapers and watch television, but how much of
what they read or watch is political by any definition? Certainly
various opinion polls have found majorities of their respondents
claiming an interest in politics, but an interest falls far short of
active participation. About 7 per cent of the adult population in
Britain are individual members of a political party, but the active
members constitute less than one-half per cent of the population.

Just under half the population are members of an organisation such as a trade union or other interest group, but the majority of these are active only to the extent of paying their membership subscriptions.

This leads to the argument that the level of participation is not as important as the *opportunity* to participate. There need be no assumption that non-participation indicates satisfaction or consent, merely that provision of the opportunity is a sufficient condition for the existence of democracy. This normally means not only the opportunity to vote, but the opportunity to express opinions and organise political activity freely and openly. Such opportunities can be provided by law, but some observers assert that the legal guarantee of these and other rights is not enough. The right to vote is of little use if its exercise is subject to bribery, corruption, personation and intimidation. The right of free speech and freedom of association are of little consolation if they never achieve anything or if people fear to use them. Economic and social deprivation, it is argued, can effectively nullify legal rights. Money and education may create a situation like that found in George Orwell's *Animal Farm*: "All animals are equal, but some animals are more equal than others".[1] It is not only a question that material advantage may provide political advantage, but a question of a consciousness and willingness to make use of the opportunities legally provided: the man whose prime concern is to survive until tomorrow may have little time for (or indeed knowledge of) his democratic rights or opportunities unless he regards them as relevant to his survival. It is not necessary to argue that democracy can only exist in a state of economic and social equality (though some would adhere to this view), but who is to say what level of economic and social *inequality* is incompatible with democracy?

Even if economic and social conditions do not frustrate the opportunity to participate they may seriously affect the operation of the democratic principle in another important way. Democracy is sometimes equated with majority rule and devices such as the referendum and elections may be used to determine majority opinion. The logic of majority rule appears irrefutable if democracy is defined as government involving popular consent and control, all the more so where such consent and control can be expressed through the ballot box. Yet much depends on the nature of the majority. Economic and social conditions may be such that there exists in a society a permanent or semipermanent majority whose will always prevails because of its numerical superiority. If that majority is based on ethnic or religious divisions, for example, then minority groups may find themselves economically, socially and politically at a permanent disadvantage. This fear of a sectional majority was the "tyranny of the majority" which led the Founding Fathers of the United States to incorporate a number of antimajoritarian devices in the American Constitution, notably the separation of the executive, legislative and judicial powers. The sectional majority is all the more to be feared for being able to assert that its power is legitimate by virtue of being the majority. It could be argued, for instance, that the Catholic minority in Northern Ireland has been subject to the tyranny of the Protestant majority. Certainly Catholics have been economically, socially and politically disadvantaged by the Protestant majority in Ulster. Philosophers like John Stuart Mill also feared the tyranny of the "ignorant" majority over the "enlightened" minority of citizens in society, and this made him pessimistic about the ultimate effects of democracy. Mill took the view that there were circumstances in which it would be wrong for the will of the majority to prevail, such as where the majority sought to use its numerical superiority as a justification for persecuting the minority. Mill also questioned whether the majority should prevail in matters on which it was inadequately informed.

Sectional majorities can and do exist, but fears of the "ignorant" majority may be exaggerated in that it is an assumption that all members of the "ignorant" majority will hold the same opinion. Moreover, public opinion is often fragmented and divisions of opinion are not necessarily related to how well-informed people are. Everyone is a member of the "ignorant" majority on one or more issues and "enlightenment" is no one's prerogative. What is at question is not whether anyone, well-informed or ill-informed, should be allowed to express an opinion, but whether that opinion should prevail if it constitutes the majority opinion. The majoritarian version of democracy argues that the will of the majority must prevail, but that it is open to any minority to seek a change in opinion and to persuade the majority of its point of view. Furthermore, in reply to those who point to the "ignorant" majority and fear the tyranny of the majority, the majoritarian simply argues that the consequences of the will of the majority must be accepted if democracy is to exist and that the only remedy for any ignorance and prejudice among the majority lies in educating, informing and communicating with the majority: those who cannot persuade the majority do not deserve to prevail.

Unfortunately, it is seldom as simple as this. There are, as we have seen, practical difficulties about ascertaining the will of the majority, but even if these practical difficulties were overcome it is open to question whether a majority opinion exists on every conceivable issue. What if there is no majority, should the will of the largest organised minority prevail? Moreover, we cannot assume that all issues can be reduced to a choice of alternatives, yet the wider the choice the less likely any one proposal is to receive the approval of an absolute majority. The relative majority may be an acceptable alternative, for some issues at least, but at what point does a relative majority become democratically unacceptable – 45 per cent, 40 per cent, 35 per cent? Majority rule, whether relative or absolute, takes no account of the intensity, saliency or consistency of opinions, nor of whether opinion is well-informed or ill-informed, for it assumes that the will of the majority is all that matters, however that majority is constituted. The principle of one man, one vote, one value is enshrined in the British electoral system. If there are disadvantages in allowing elections to be determined on such a basis then they are disadvantages that must be accepted; proposals for giving some electors a greater say than others are politically dead. One man, one vote, one value is the accepted and acceptable basis of conducting elections.

It is all too easy, however, to equate this same principle with *one man, one opinion, one value*. In electoral terms this may be so, but it does not justify extending the principle to all political decisions. It is obvious that in many matters, perhaps most, some people's opinions are more important than others', sometimes because they alone have the requisite expertise, sometimes because their consent is crucial to any solution, sometimes because they feel more strongly about it than other people. Who can say who should prevail? Should the miners alone decide what is to be done in the coal industry? But we, the public, are, directly or indirectly, consumers of coal. Should the doctors determine the policy of the National Health Service? But we, the public, are all patients, past, present or future. Few would advocate that the views of miners or doctors in their respective fields be ignored, and it would seem sensible at least to listen, but how much notice should be taken of what they have to say? Things which affect only miners or doctors can, perhaps, be safely left to miners and doctors, but who should prevail if the wishes of a majority of the miners or a majority of doctors conflicts with the wishes of a majority of the public?

To attempt to reduce democracy to a single rule, such as the will of the majority, robs it of its necessary flexibility: democracy demands compromise, not intransigence, negotiation, not ultimatums, cooperation not obstruction. Nor is democracy the sum of various political, social and economic rights; these are necessary but not sufficient conditions for the existence of democracy. Such rights may in fact exist quite independently from democracy and historically have done so. Freedom of speech, freedom of association, freedom from arbitrary arrest and the provision of varying degrees of social and economic equality do not necessarily involve popular consent or control. Moreover, even where it exists, popular consent and control can, in some instances, be specific and direct – notably through elections and referenda – but it cannot be absolute and continuous. Democracy must be content with machinery which makes governments sensitive and responsive to public opinion and which offers the public the opportunity of calling the government to account. This also means that democracy must be seen as involving on the part of government and governed an attitude of mind which embraces a willingness to compromise, to negotiate, to cooperate, to respect the rights and opinions of others and, at times, to let them prevail whether or not they constitute a majority.

Democracy, however, is ultimately a matter of opinion, for as Edmund Burke wrote: "If any ask me what free government is, I answer, that for any practical purpose, it is what the people think so."[2]

Is Britain democratic?

Englishmen were claiming various rights long before democracy was a meaningful part of their political vocabulary: Magna Carta the Petition of Right and the Bill of Rights are not democratic documents, even if they have become part of the liberal democratic tradition. Magna Carta is an essentially feudal document concerned with feudal rights. The Petition of Right is largely concerned with the proper exercise by the King of rights which were feudal in origin. The Bill of Rights reasserts what were regarded as existing rights and is a statement of the constitutional situation following the flight of James II and the accession to the throne of William III and Mary. It was the culmination of a prolonged period of constitutional dispute and change and marks the establishment of a constitutional monarchy, but the Bill of Rights is hardly the foundation stone of democracy. Similarly, the extension of the franchise in the Representation of the People Acts of 1832, 1867, 1884, 1918 and 1928 may have been necessary preconditions for democracy or its extension, but they did not establish it. The welfare state may have created conditions in which democracy can grow and flourish, but if democracy needs the welfare state it does not follow that the welfare state needs democracy.

If Britain is to any extent a democracy it is because machinery has been developed and conditions created which enable some degree of popular consent and control to be exercised. Democracy cannot be equated with majority rule as expressed through elections since no party normally wins a majority of the votes cast, let alone the support of a majority of those eligible to vote. In a less specific sense, however, majority rule may be said to prevail inasmuch as the majority of the electorate appears to accept the legitimacy of government by the party winning a majority of seats in the House of Commons, which is usually the party with the most votes. But with regard to specific policies it is often impossible to judge whether they enjoy the support of a majority, unless passivity and silence are equated with consent.

There are, as we have seen, various ways by which public opinion may be elicited and can make itself felt, but we have also seen that public opinion is a complex phenomenon which cannot be expressed solely through the ballot box. The introduction and widespread use of the referendum and the initiative would still leave vast areas of policy and public concern untouched for there is a practical limit to the number of referenda which could be held and the number of initiatives undertaken. In practice referenda and initiatives would exist largely as machinery of appeal in anticipation of or against government decisions. There would remain the greater part of public policy, which would not stimulate such appeals to the people.

It can be argued that democracy, far from being limited to the ballot box, can find expression through pressure groups, political parties, the mass media, opinion polls, demonstrations, petitions, letters to ministers and to civil servants and other officials, and, by no means least, through Parliament. *Within* organisations such as parties and pressure groups some machinery may exist for ascertaining the will of the majority of their members on certain issues, but for the most part the contribution to democracy of such organisations and devices is more subtle and less exact than the counting of heads. Some heads will count for more than others, for these organisations and devices provide a forum for expert, informed and affected opinion which may claim as much right to be heard as general opinion. It remains a matter of opinion, however, whether, having been heard, expert, informed or affected opinion should prevail.

What happens in practice in Britain is that government listens, though this is not to deny that it sometimes appears to be hard of hearing, and decides in the knowledge that it may be called to account for its decisions. However imperfectly, provision does exist for the expression of opinion and even though public opinion may be ignored some of the time it is not ignored all of the time. Furthermore, its very expression is a form of control, for the government knows that in due course the public will have the opportunity at a general election of passing judgment on its conduct of affairs. Sections of the public also have the opportunity to pronounce judgment at by-elections, while the government is subject to continuous scrutiny and frequent criticism in the mass media and ministers are expected to defend their actions publicly, all of which facilitates popular control.

Politics, however, is not synonymous with democracy and undue emphasis on democracy may make the conduct of politics extremely difficult, even impossible. Popular consent and control must, in the words of some Victorian constitutional legislation, be balanced, with the need for "peace, order and good government". Those in government, elected and appointed, national and local, have a task which ignores political reality at its peril. The effectiveness of government is at least as important as popular consent and control, and effective government demands that decisions be made in the light of as many factors as possible. There may be occasions when effective government must be tempered by the needs of democracy, but there are also times when democracy must be tempered by the need for effective government. No government can operate effectively in a situation in which it must be certain that every policy enjoys the consent of the governed before it can be implemented; and the politician who pleads the public right or wrong preaches a dangerous doctrine.

Neither consent nor control is or can be continuous. Consent must be seen in terms of providing opportunities for the expression of opinion, an acceptance on the part of the government that it should be sensitive to opinion, and not simply as securing specific consent to particular policies. Control must be seen in terms of providing means by which the government can be called to account, an acceptance on the part of the government that it should explain and defend its proposals and actions, and not as direct and frequent participation in the decision-making process. Democracy exists not when a majority is satisfied with a decision that the government has taken, but when it is satisfied with the *manner* in which it was taken.

If, as we have argued, democracy is ultimately a matter of opinion, the question whether Britain is democratic can only be answered by the public. In 1973 a Gallup Poll found that 65 per cent of its respondents thought Britain was a democratic country, 19 per cent did not, and 16 per cent were "don't knows". But the same poll also found that 71 per cent of the respondents did not think they had enough say in the way the government ran the country and successive polls have shown that a majority of the electorate think that certain issues should be decided by referenda (Social Surveys (Gallup), February 1973). Another poll conducted in 1969 produced similar results and there is no reason to believe that opinion has moved significantly away from such a view. These polls would suggest that there is a widespread feeling that Britain is a democratic country, but an equally widespread feeling that it is not democratic enough. The support for the devolution of power to Scotland and Wales and for the introduction of proportional representation are further evidence of this, but the role that Parliament could play in extending democracy should not be forgotten.

Parliament and the public

Parliament suffers from public ignorance of what it does. We have seen that the survey conducted on behalf of the Top Salaries Review Board found widespread ignorance about MPs' salaries and the hours they worked. The survey conducted in preparation for the Granada Television series *The State of the Nation* found that although

60 per cent of its respondents knew the maximum number of years that could elapse between general elections and 78 per cent could name the party of their MP, only 53 per cent could actually name their MP, only 25 per cent were aware that Parliament does *not* appoint the Cabinet, and only 22 per cent could give an accurate estimate of the number of MPs in the House of Commons. In spite of the fact that 71 per cent of the respondents claimed to be very or fairly interested in what goes on in Parliament and that 55 per cent were prepared to say that Parliament works very or fairly well, 77 per cent said they knew nothing or not very much about Parliament. These results appear to be part of a wider ignorance of the working of politics in Britain, for when respondents were asked to cite the three institutions most important in law-making 63 per cent nominated Parliament, 28 per cent the courts, 25 per cent the police, and only 24 per cent the Cabinet, 23 per cent political parties and a mere 6 per cent the Civil Service.[3] It is likely that these latter replies were affected by the use of the phrase "law-making", but even so they hardly indicate a widespread understanding of the relationship between the government and Parliament. Yet in 1983 Gallup found that 54 per cent of its respondents had a "great deal" or "quite a lot" of confidence in Parliament (Social Surveys [Gallup], April 1983).

It is possible that public knowledge and understanding of Parliament has been increased by the broadcasting of its proceedings. This began with a four-week experiment in 1975 of broadcasting Commons proceedings and was followed by the regular broadcasting of the proceedings of both Houses from 1978. These broadcasts were confined to sound, however, and apart from televising the State Opening of Parliament, it was not until January 1985 that the television cameras were admitted, and then only by the House of Lords; the House of Commons chose to await the outcome of the Lords' experience. Opinion on the impact of sound broadcasting has been sharply divided between those who argued that the periodic noisiness, even rowdiness, of the Commons has caused Parliament to suffer a fall in public esteem, and those who argue that public understanding has been increased by hearing the politicians argue their cases rather than relying on second-hand reporting. Similar arguments rage over the likely effect of television, yet much depends on *what* is heard and seen: the rowdy and the dramatic needs to be contrasted with the quietly effective and the mundane, the work of the chamber with the work of the committees, the partisan with the non-partisan activity. All too frequently selectivity, deliberately or otherwise, can give a misleading impression, to which the only effective answer may be continuous broadcasting on a special channel.

Public knowledge and understanding of Parliament may seem to have little relevance to its effectiveness in carrying out its role of scrutinising the activities of the government, but Parliament offers the best opportunity of trying to ensure that the government pays attention to public opinion and that the government is accountable to the public, and the more the public understands Parliament the better use they will be able to make of it.

Parliament, as we have seen, is not a microcosm of the nation, nor should it be regarded as some sort of permanent or semi-permanent sample survey of public opinion, but it can act as a channel for and a filter of public opinion in the widest sense of the term. Most MPs keep in touch with or are made aware of public opinion in their constituencies and elsewhere on a wide range of issues; most MPs have contacts with various pressure groups and other sources of expert and informed opinion; and if public opinion – expert, informed, affected or general – is strong enough on any matter it will almost certainly find some expression in Parliament. The expression of opinion through Parliament is no guarantee of success, but why should it be? Parliament, at least, does have the advantage of being close to the centre of power and decision and through its members it is there all the time: the public does not have to wait until the mass media or the opinion polls focus on an issue before opinion can find expression. Of course, MPs, because of their particular political beliefs, eschew some sources of opinion and information, but what one MP rejects another is likely to accept. MPs articulate and aggregate public opinion; they also interpret it. A House of Commons which is no more than an echo of public opinion is failing, not serving, the public: Parliament exists to question, not to echo.

The public is best served by Parliament fulfilling its role of making the government accountable, accountable not in the constitutional sense to Parliament, but to the public. We noted earlier that Parliament is more effective in dealing with political "blow-ups" than with the more mundane business of routine accountability. The potential exists, however, notably in the form of select committees, but there are limits to what these committees can achieve. And Parliament's scrutiny of legislation is hampered by its general inability to hear expert evidence at the committee stage. Moreover, while MPs have enjoyed a marked improvement in their services and facilities since the mid-1960s, they still lack a level of facilities that most businessmen take for granted. Similarly, in spite of the excellent services provided by the House of Commons Library, a more comprehensive information and research service is necessary if MPs are to be adequately equipped to question and criticise ministers. Such developments do not depend on public understanding and support, but such understanding and support would do much to bring them about. It has been said that people get the government they deserve. Perhaps the public gets the Parliament it deserves, but the public can survive without Parliament: can an effective Parliament survive without the public?

Notes and references

Chapter 1. Introduction

1. Bernard Crick, *In Defence of Politics*, rev. edn, Penguin Books, 1964, p. 167.

Chapter 2. Parliament and politics

1. Erskine May, *Treatise on the Law, Privileges, Proceedings and Usage of Parliament*, 20th edn, ed. Sir Charles Gordon, Butterworth, 1983, p. 3.
2. The formula is slightly different for the annual Finance Act, Private Acts and acts passed under the special procedures of the Parliament Acts, 1911 and 1949.
3. A.V. Dicey, *The Law of the Constitution*, 10th edn, Macmillan, 1959, pp. 39–40.

Chapter 3. Parliament and its functions

1. *Review Body on Top Salaries: Review of Parliamentary Pay and Allowances* (The Plowden Report), Vol. 2: Surveys and Studies, Cmnd. 8881–II, May 1983, Section 1, Tables 6 and 7.
2. *Plowden Report*, Section 1, Tables 3 and 4.
3. *Plowden Report*, Section 1, Tables 16 and 17.
4. Anthony Barker and Michael Rush, *The Member of Parliament and His Information*, Allen & Unwin, 1970, Appendix 3, Tables 3, 4 and 15.

Chapter 4. Parliament and representation

1. A.H. Birch, *Representative and Responsible Government*, Allen & Unwin, London, 1964, pp. 14–16.
2. *The Works of Edmund Burke*, George Bell, 1883, I, p. 446–7.

3. *Ibid*, I, p. 447.
4. *Ibid*, I, p. 375.

Chapter 5.   Parliament and policy

1. Birch, *Representative and Responsible Government*, pp. 17–18.
2. J.A.G. Griffith, *The Parliamentary Scrutiny of Government Bills*, Allen & Unwin, 1974.
3. Granada Television, *The State of the Nation: Parliament*, London, 1973, pp. 153, 159–60, 179, and 193.

Chapter 6.   Parliament and public opinion

1. *Review Body on Top Salaries: Ministers of the Crown and members of Parliament* (The Boyle Report), Cmnd. 4836, December 1971, p. 11 and Appendix B.

Chapter 7.   Parliament and democracy

1. George Orwell, *Animal Farm*, Secker & Warburg, 1945, p. 105.
2. *The Works of Edmund Burke*, vol. II, p. 29.
3. *The State of the Nation: Parliament*, p. 202.

Further Reading

General

It is important not to divorce Parliament from the political issues of the day and this is best achieved by following events through the press, radio and television. Newspapers, especially *The Times*, *Guardian*, *Daily Telegraph*, *Sunday Times*, *Sunday Telegraph* and *Observer*, provide an invaluable running commentary on political issues and parliamentary events. Periodicals, such the *Economist*, the *New Statesman* and the *Spectator*, provide comment in greater depth. Since January 1985 selected debates in the House of Lords have been televised and it may not be long before the House of Commons is persuaded to admit the cameras. There is, however, no regular television programme devoted to Parliament, but current affairs programmes, such as the BBC's "Panorama", "Newsnight", "Question Time" and "This Week, Next Week", ITV's "World in Action", "TV Eye" and "Weekend World", and Channel 4's "A Week in Politics", perform a similar function to weekly periodicals. Radio coverage has undoubtedly been enhanced by the broadcasting of extracts from parliamentary debates and there are a number of highly relevant programmes, including "Today in Parliament", "Yesterday in Parliament", "The Week in Westminster", "Inside Parliament" and "Talking Politics". A number of Open University programmes, notably "Decision-Making in Britain", are very instructive and often include contributions from individuals directly involved in politics, such as the Prime Minister, other ministers, MPs, civil servants and so on. There are also a number of academic journals which regularly contain articles on parliamentary studies. These include *Parliamentary Affairs*, *Political Quarterly*, *The Parliamentarian*, *Public Administration* and *Public Law*.

Chapter 1. Introduction

The number and variety of books on the nature of politics and the problems of political studies is enormous and much depends on the tastes of the reader.

The following provide a good cross-section of different styles and approaches: Bernard Crick, *In Defence of Politics* (Penguin Books, 2nd edn. 1982); J.D.B. Miller, *The Nature of Politics* (Penguin Books, 1965); Maurice Duverger, *The Idea of Politics* (English edn. Methuen, 1966); Harold D. Lasswell, *Who Gets What, When, How* (originally published Chicago 1930, new edn. Meridan Books, 1958); and W.J.M. Mackenzie, *Politics and Social Science* (Penguin Books, 1967).

Chapter 2.   Parliament and politics

General texts, such as J.P. Mackintosh, *The Government and Politics of Britain*, revised and updated by Peter G. Richards (Hutchinson, 5th edn. 1982); A.H. Hanson and Malcolm Walles, *Governing Britain* (Fontana, 3rd edn. 1980); A.H. Birch, *The British System of Government* (Allen & Unwin, 4th edn. 1980); and Michael Rush, *Parliamentary Government in Britain* (Pitman, 1981) provide useful general surveys of British politics. A more exhaustive account can be found in R.M. Punnett, *British Government and Politics* (Heinemann, 4th edn. 1980) and a Marxist view in Colin Leys, *Politics in Britain: An Introduction* (Heinemann, 1981).

Kenneth Mackenzie, *The English Parliament* (Penguin Books, 1959) is a short but useful introduction to the evolution of Parliament, while the best longer work on this subject is A.F. Pollard, *The Evolution of Parliament* (Longman, 2nd revised edn. 1926). In addition, there are standard texts on constitutional history, such as Sir D.L. Keir, *The Constitutional History of Modern Britain* (A. & C. Black, 1964) and S.B. Chrimes, *English Constitutional History* (Oxford University Press, 1965). Textbooks on constitutional law, such as O. Hood Phillips and Paul Jackson, *Constitutional and Administrative Law* (Sweet & Maxwell, 9th edn. 1977) and E.C.S. Wade and G.G. Phillips, *Constitutional and Administrative Law* (Longman, 6th edn. 1978), provide a useful legal background.

G. Marshall and G.C. Moodie, *Some Problems of the Constitution* (Hutchinson, 1961); H.J. Laski, *Parliamentary Government in England* (Allen & Unwin, 1958); H.J. Laski, *Reflections on the Constitution* (Manchester University Press, 1962); L.S. Amery, *Thoughts on the Constitution* (Oxford University Press, 1964); Ian Gilmour, *The Body Politic* (Hutchinson, 1969); Max Nicholson, *The System* (Hodder & Stoughton, 1967); and Nevil Johnson, *In Search of the Constitution* (Pergamon, 1977 and Methuen, 1980) are stimulating commentaries on the British constitution and political system.

Chapter 3.   Parliament and its functions

The standard text on Parliament is Sir Ivor Jennings, *Parliament* (Cambridge University Press, 2nd edn. 1969), which, though out of date, offers a valuable recent historical perspective. Eric Taylor, *The House of Commons at Work* (Macmillan, 9th edn. 1979) provides a short, reliable account of Parliament's functions and procedures, and Kenneth Bradshaw and David Pring, *Parliament and Congress* (Quartet Books, rev. edn. 1981) is a more exhaustive treatment and provides an interesting comparative perspective with American legislative practice.

Bernard Crick, *The Reform of Parliament* (Weidenfeld & Nicolson, 2nd rev. edn. 1968) is a stimulating and refreshing look at the work of Parliament and Peter G. Richards, *The Backbenchers* (Faber, 1972) is an extremely readable and thoughtful book on the role of the MP. A detailed historical perspective can be found in S.A. Walkland (ed.), *The House of Commons in the Twentieth Century* (Oxford University Press, 1979) and detailed accounts of various aspects of parliamentary work can be found in David Coombes, *The Member of Parliament and the Administration* (an account of the work of the Select Committee on Nationalised Industries) (Allen & Unwin, 1966); Nevil Johnson, *Parliament and the Administration: the Estimates Committee, 1945–65* (Allen & Unwin, 1966); Anthony Barker and Michael Rush, *The Member of Parliament and His Information* (Allen & Unwin, 1970); Ann Robinson, *Parliament and Public Spending* (Heinemann, 1978); Michael Rush and Malcolm Shaw (eds.), *The House of Commons: Services and Facilities* (Allen & Unwin, 1974); David Judge, *Backbench Specialisation in the House of Commons* (Heinemann, 1981); Michael Rush (ed.), *The House of Commons: Services and Facilities, 1972–1982* (Policy Studies Institute, 1983); and Gavin Drewry (ed.), *The New Select Committees: A Study of the 1979 Reforms* (Oxford University Press, 1985). Finally, a discussion by MPs of their perceptions of their roles can be found in Anthony King (ed.), *British Members of Parliament: A Self-Portrait* (Macmillan, 1974).

It is also instructive to browse through *Hansard* (verbatim debates) and look at parliamentary papers, comprising reports and other documents presented to Parliament, the bills it considers and the reports produced by select committees, which give some idea of the workload and how much "bumph" MPs are faced with.

Chapter 4. Parliament and representation

The best book on the concept of representation is A.H. Birch, *Representative and Responsible Government* (Allen & Unwin, 1964). Peter Pulzer, *Political Representation and Elections in Britain* (Allen & Unwin, 3rd edn. 1975) and Iain Maclean, *Elections* (Longman, 2nd edn. 1980) provide excellent discussions of elections, electoral behaviour and the problems of representation. W.J.M. Mackenzie, *Free Elections* (Allen & Unwin, 1958) and E. Lakeman, *How Democracies Vote* (Faber, 4th edn. 1974) are exhaustive accounts of different electoral systems, whilst a more polemical view is provided by S.E.

Finer (ed.), *Adversary Politics and Electoral Reform* (Anthony Wigram, 1975). Details of the socio-economic backgrounds and career patterns of MPs can be found in Michael Rush, "The Members of Parliament" in S.A. Walkland (ed.), *The House of Commons in the Twentieth Century* (Oxford University Press, 1979) and up-to-date information is provided in the Nuffield Election Series (Macmillan) and Andrew Roth, *The Business Background of MPs* (Parliamentary Profiles Ltd.), both published after each general election. The process by which MPs are selected is described and discussed in Michael Rush, *The Selection of Parliamentary Candidates* (Nelson, 1969) and Alison Young, *The Reselection of MPs* (Heinemann, 1983) deals with more recent developments in the selection of candidates.

Chapter 5.   Parliament and policy

A general account of policy formation in Britain can be found in J.J. Richardson, *The Policy-Making Process* (Routledge & Kegan Paul, 1969), whilst R.G.S. Brown and David R. Steel, *The Administrative Process in Britain* (Methuen, 2nd edn. 1979) is a useful account of the role of the civil service. The role of the Prime Minister and the Cabinet is described and discussed in Michael Rush, *The Cabinet and Policy Formation* (Longman, 1984).

A useful discussion of Parliament's role in policy-making can be found in Ronald Butt, *The Power of Parliament* (Constable, 2nd edn. 1969). Parliament's legislative role is admirably described and discussed in S.A. Walkland, *The Legislative Process in Britain* (Allen & Unwin, 1968) and in much greater detail in J.A.G. Griffith, *Parliamentary Scrutiny of Government Bills* (Allen & Unwin, 1974) and Ivor Burton and Gavin Drewry, *Legislation and Public Policy: Public Bills in the 1970–74 Parliament* (Macmillan, 1981).

G. Wootton, *Pressure Politics in Contemporary Britain* (Lexington Books, 1978) and Geoffrey Alderman, *Pressure Groups and Government in Great Britain* (Longman, 1984) are good general accounts of pressure group activity, whilst there is a variety of studies of particular groups and issues, including H.H. Wilson, *Pressure Group: the Campaign for Commercial Television* (Secker and Warburg, 1961); J.B. Christoph, *Capital Punishment and British Politics* (Allen & Unwin, 1962); P. Self and H. Storing, *The State and the Farmer* (Allen & Unwin, 1962); C. Driver, *The Disarmers* (Hodder & Stoughton, 1964); Malcolm Joel Barnett, *The Politics of Legislation: The Rent Act, 1957* (Weidenfeld & Nicolson, 1969); William Plowden, *The Motor-Car and British Politics, 1896–1970* (Bodley Head, 1971); David McKie, *A Sadly Mismanaged Affair: A Political History of the Third London Airport* (Croom Helm, 1973); B. Frost (ed.), *The Tactics of Pressure* (dealing with a number of pressure group campaigns) (Galliard, 1975); D.F. Macdonald,

The State and the Trade Unions (Macmillan, 2nd edn. 1976); E. Ashby and M. Anderson, *The Politics of Clean Air* (Oxford University Press, 1981).

The edited transcript of the Granada Television Series "The State of the Nation: Parliament" (July 1973) provides invaluable insights into the work of a standing committee of the House of Commons on a public bill, a discussion of the problems of parliamentary scrutiny (in the form of a select committee inquiry), and a debate, on parliamentary lines, of various proposals for parliamentary reform.

Chapter 6.   Parliament and public opinion

The best short book on the concept of public opinion is Robert Lane and David O. Sears, *Public Opinion* (Prentice-Hall, 1964). Cecil S. Emden, *The People and the Constitution* (Oxford Uniersity Press, 2nd edn. 1956) gives a good historical perspective of public opinion. R. Hodder-Williams, *Public Opinion Polls and British Politics* (Routledge & Kegan Paul, 1970) and F. Teer and J.D. Spence, *Political Opinion Polls* (Hutchinson, 1973) provide a useful discussion of public opinion and the working of opinion polls, whilst L.J. Macfarlane, *Issues in British Politics since 1945* (Longman, 2nd edn. 1981) is a valuable compilation of public opinion on major political issues in the post-war period. Two of the major opinion polls in Britain publish monthly results in the *Gallup Political Index* and NOP's *Political, Social and Economic Review*. In addition these and other polls are published regularly in several national newspapers.

A discussion of the role of the press in Britain can be found in Colin Seymour-Ure, *The Press, Politics and the Public* (Methuen, 1968) and of the role of television in Jay Blumler and Denis McQuail, *Television in Politics: Its Uses and Influence* (Faber, 1968), and of both in Colin Seymour-Ure, *The Political Impact of the Mass Media* (Constable 1974).

Chapter 7.   Parliament and democracy

An exhaustive treatment of the subject of democracy can be found in Barry Holden, *The Nature of Democracy* (Nelson, 1974). Bernard Crick, *In Defence of Politics* (especially Chap. 3), provides a stimulating view of the subject and Peter Pulzer, *Political Representation and Elections in Britain* (Chap. 1 and 5) is a useful discussion of the problems involved in democratic theory and practice. A more detailed study of democracy and social policy can be found in S.I. Benn and R.S. Peters, *Social Principles and the Democratic State* (Allen & Unwin, 2nd edn. 1965), and a stimulating American perspective is provided in Robert A. Dahl, *A Preface to Democratic Theory* (University of Chicago Press, 1956).

Index